YOU'RE ALL TALK

Rob Drummond is Professor of Sociolinguistics at Manchester Metropolitan University, where he researches and teaches about the relationship between how we speak and who we are. He recently completed a large project exploring the accents and dialects of Greater Manchester, touring the region in his Accent Van. He appears regularly on radio and TV talking about language-related issues and spent some time as the 'resident linguist' on BBC Radio 3's *The Verb*, as well as appearing on the BBC *Breakfast* sofa.

@RobDrummond
robdrummond.co.uk

Rob Drummond

YOU'RE ALL TALK

Why We Are What We Speak

SCRIBE

Melbourne | London | Minneapolis

For Lynda, Maya, Cassia, and Isaac.

Scribe Publications
18–20 Edward St, Brunswick, Victoria 3056, Australia
2 John St, Clerkenwell, London, WC1N 2ES, United Kingdom
3754 Pleasant Ave, Suite 100, Minneapolis, Minnesota 55409, USA

First published by Scribe 2023
This edition published 2025

Copyright © Rob Drummond 2023

All rights reserved. Without limiting the rights under copyright reserved above, no part of this publication may be reproduced, stored in or introduced into a retrieval system, or transmitted, in any form or by any means (electronic, mechanical, photocopying, recording or otherwise) without the prior written permission of the publishers of this book.

The moral rights of the author have been asserted.

Typeset in Adobe Caslon Pro by the publishers

Printed and bound in the UK by CPI Group (UK) Ltd, Croydon CR0 4YY

Scribe is committed to the sustainable use of natural resources and the use of paper products made responsibly from those resources.

978 1 922585 45 5 (Australian edition)
978 1 917189 12 5 (UK edition)
978 1 761385 28 5 (ebook)

Catalogue records for this book are available from the National Library of Australia and the British Library.

scribepublications.com.au
scribepublications.co.uk
scribepublications.com

Contents

Preface 1

CHAPTER 1
Why are there so many accents? 17

CHAPTER 2
Why we are what we speak 49

CHAPTER 3
**Prejudice and discrimination:
how accents can hold us back** 81

CHAPTER 4
**Style-shifting and code-switching:
why does Mum sound so posh on the phone?** 145

CHAPTER 5
Soon we'll just be grunting to one another 193

Postscript 221

Glossary 225

Notes 231

Acknowledgements 249

Preface

In April 2019, US politician Alexandria Ocasio-Cortez gave a speech at a convention in New Jersey, in which she reflected on her humble background, and the dignity and pride found in traditionally working-class jobs. However, what made headlines was not Ocasio-Cortez's powerful words — 'There is nothing wrong with being a working person in the United States of America' — but rather the way in which she delivered them. Ocasio-Cortez, who is of Puerto Rican descent, was accused of faking an African American way of speaking to address the predominantly Black audience. Political and media critics piled on to claim she was patronising her audience by putting on an accent that was not her own, and even that she was racist for doing so. Ocasio-Cortez swiftly faced down these accusations by pointing out on Twitter: 'I am from the Bronx. I act & talk like it, *especially* when I'm fired up and especially when I'm home.' She said that she was simply doing what came naturally to her.

In 2013, another politician, Britain's George Osborne, had been similarly criticised about a speech he gave at a supermarket warehouse in Kent. Apparently aware that his voice sounds quite 'posh', Osborne seems to have tried to make his speech closer — in his mind at least — to the likely accents of his audience members, resulting in what is often termed a 'mockney' (fake cockney) accent, including dropped 'h's and missing 't's. This was ridiculed in the British media: '"MOCKNEY" GEORGE OSBORNE BACKS THE BRIDDISH WHO WANNA WORK'. Unlike Ocasio-Cortez, Osborne did not claim any ownership of this way of speaking, and we don't know how aware he was at the time that he was doing it. But the fact is, he did it.

So, was it right that Osborne be ridiculed? Was Ocasio-Cortez's justification convincing? Should they both have stuck with their more familiar accents? A lot of people thought so. But those very same people — in fact almost all of us — most likely make extremely similar linguistic adjustments every day.

Being judgy

Have you ever made a judgement about a person based on the way they speak (or the words they use — 'judgy', for example)? Perhaps you overheard somebody talking and thought 'they sound friendly/boring/intelligent/rude'. Or maybe you met someone and didn't consciously think about their voice at all, but came away with the impression that they were kind, or nervous, or smug, or aloof, despite actually knowing very little about them. Perhaps you heard someone speaking with an accent that you associate with a particular person, or with certain characteristics? Maybe it was the radio presenter with the 'posh' voice who sounds so calm and intelligent; the colleague who reminds you of that comedian you like from somewhere in Yorkshire; the group of teenagers on the bus who have that accent you can't quite place but which sets your teeth on edge; the friendly American (is she American or Canadian?) woman with the big dog at the park; that rude bloke who lives at number 5 who sounds like he thinks he's better than everyone else; the bored shop assistant who really needs to work on their enunciation. We all form judgements about people in part, or maybe almost entirely, based on how they speak. If you're listening to this as an audiobook, it's probably happening right now!

And it's not just other people's voices that we can be judgemental about. When was the last time you were aware of your own way of speaking? Maybe it's something you give very little thought to, or perhaps you consider it every time you open your mouth. You might be the sort of person who consciously and deliberately adjusts the way you speak depending on where you are and how you want to come across. Perhaps it is even part of your job to do so: if you work on the reception desk of a prestigious law firm and have been told to answer the phone in a particular way so as to maintain the preferred company identity, for example; or as a youth worker who knows precisely how to adapt your tone in order to engage with, and gain the trust of, the young people you work with. You may have experienced people explicitly making judgements about your voice, like the footballer turned sports presenter Alex Scott who was pulled up on Twitter for not pronouncing her 'g's or UK journalist and TV presenter Steph McGovern, who was once offered £20 to put towards elocution lessons from a viewer who took a dislike to her Middlesbrough accent (in which *play* sounds like 'pleh' and *better* can sound like 'betta').[1] But what effect does such criticism have? Does it make someone try to lessen those features that stand out, or does it make them pronounce them even more strongly in defiance? Maybe you've felt it necessary to change the way you speak in order to 'fit in' with a particular environment, especially if your accent is routinely viewed as being less prestigious. As a result, lots of us will notice our speech quickly changing back again when we chat to friends and family from where we grew up. Although you might be the sort of person who feels they pretty much have one way of speaking and this is it: take it or leave it. Doing anything different would be a betrayal of who you really are. Wouldn't it?

This is me. And this. Oh, and this.

This is a book about the relationship between how we speak and who we are. More precisely, it's a book about the role of spoken language,[2] specifically English,[3] in creating all the different versions of us that we employ in our day-to-day lives. Our identities are reflected in the clothes we wear, the way we style our hair, our use of makeup (or not), our piercings and our tattoos (or not), our taste in music, our life choices, our general behaviour, and so on. And, of course, they are also reflected in our language. The way we speak can provide a lot of clues about us — where we live or where we're from, our social class, possibly even our jobs, and maybe more.

For example, who exactly am I, and how is this reflected in my voice? You may have an idea in your head of how I sound, based on my writing style and any background information gleaned from my biography. Perhaps my publisher has splashed out on a headshot of me looking scholarly, yet approachable, as if this is my effortless everyday demeanour, to provide you with further clues. If you had been sitting next to me as I wrote this preface before heading off to teach, you'd have seen me wearing jeans, boots, a shirt, and a linen jacket, with a bald shaved head and greying beard. What would this suggest about how I might sound, and who I might be? When I spoke, you'd have heard my fairly 'standard' (we'll revisit this term later) British English voice and my lack of a 'regional' (we'll revisit this too) accent, and this, coupled with my appearance and anything else you know about me, would have likely led you to form a pretty accurate impression of a middle-aged, white, educated, middle-class man from the south-east of England — perhaps a teacher of some kind. If we spent longer than ten minutes together, you might start to form a more detailed view of who I am, based on what I was saying and how I was behaving. But all of this would happen in relation to what information you had initially gained from my appearance and from my speech: first impressions can be powerful. If you'd met me instead on holiday, or when I was doing something that was out of my comfort zone, or when I was losing patience with my kids, you might have formed a completely different impression of who I was.

> Of course, this perception of my identity only works if you are familiar with the context and perhaps the culture in which our meeting took place. If you aren't from the UK, you might not be able to place my accent, and my clothes may signify something completely different. The point is, the links between my speech, my clothes, my behaviour, and various social characteristics such as my social class, my level of education, my job, and so on are not fixed. They don't work in the same way together to suggest an identity regardless of where I am; how we perceive that identity is entirely dependent on our knowledge and understanding of culture and context. Many of us put at least three basic identities into practice every single day: at work, with friends, and with family. We usually even have different relationships, and therefore identities, within these groups (the way you speak to your boss and your work best friend is likely not the same, for good reason). From when we are very young, we are expected to linguistically negotiate

our multiple worlds, which are already complex. We are reminded to speak a certain way when this person visits the house, but not when that person visits. We might use a particular word all the time, but suddenly when Grandma's here, Mum acts like she's appalled that we even know that it exists.

Let's imagine a typical 17-year-old in the UK in 2022, who lives with her dad and siblings, goes to sixth form college, works part time at Nando's, and spends a lot of time on TikTok. We'll call her Anya. In each context, her speech and behaviour is likely to change in relation to the expectations of the other people in the situation, and the different ways in which Anya wants to be perceived. Not everything changes, and some changes may be very subtle, but the changes that do occur help distinguish Anya's identities from one another. At college, Anya makes an effort to maintain a particular look — clothes and trainers are carefully chosen, hair and makeup is immaculate. Her style is very similar to her group of three close friends, and very different from some other groups. She also shares a language style with this close group, peppered with phrases and references from TikTok, many of which started life thousands of miles away in a completely different context. The dexterity with which she and her friends manipulate this language separates them from the other students around them, some of whom look on in thinly disguised awe, others with open contempt. In lessons, Anya's appearance is the same, but the language she uses with her friends melts away and is replaced by something more suited to the classroom. Her accent might even change slightly. Anya knows that in order to do well in this class, she has to speak in full sentences, enunciate her words, and use 'subject-specific terminology', whatever that means. This teacher won't indulge her slang (despite her knowing for a fact that he uses a lot of it himself outside the classroom, as witnessed in that video they found online), so she adjusts her speech accordingly. Later at home, the makeup disappears, the hair is tied back, and her voice shifts once more. Swearing is toned down, except for the odd mild word that tests the boundaries of what is or isn't acceptable to her dad in front of her younger sister, and family in-jokes creep in. Soon, when she finds that her Nando's uniform hasn't been washed, and is actually still on her bedroom floor, she and her dad will fall into the clichéd roles of tired parent and ungrateful teenager, with all the accompanying eye-rolling, shouting, and misunderstanding. At work the next day, Anya puts on both her physical and linguistic uniform, and reluctantly channels her Nando's persona — smiling, chatting, and politely laughing out on the floor; grimacing, conspiring, and collectively despairing behind the scenes in the kitchen; in both, confidently using the accepted Nando's jargon. After work, she goes to a friend's house where they attempt to recreate some of the latest TikTok trends. The combined distancing and protective effects of the phone, the friend's bedroom, and the opportunity to do something again and again until it's just right, allow a confidence and humour that doesn't exist anywhere else in Anya's day-to-day life. TikTok Anya is very different from classroom Anya.

But this isn't to say that there are rigid boundaries between these different Anyas, or between the different versions of you that exist at work, with friends, and at home. Rather, these identities are fluid and overlapping. And, as well as adapting in the present, these identities will also, depending on the context, change over time. As we move through our lives, we find ourselves in different situations, or in familiar situations but with a different perspective. We have different priorities, and might start to relate to people in different ways. It is unlikely that anyone in their 50s feels that they are exactly the same person as they were in their 20s. Anya at 40 will undoubtedly look back at the TikTok-famous Anya at 17 with a mixture of recognition and disbelief. As will any children she may have.

So: I speak the way I do because I am a middle-aged, white, educated, middle-class university professor from the south of England. I subtly change the way I speak in different situations because my identity is slightly different depending on the context. Alexandria Ocasio-Cortez, George Osborne, Anya, and most likely you all do the same, with varying success. But, to take things a step further, do our — very different — voices simply *reflect* our identities, or does the way we speak actually help to *create* those identities?

It's all a performance

Much in the same way that an actor will use their voice to help them perform a particular character, we too use our voices to perform who we are. I don't speak the way I speak *because* I am a middle-aged, white, middle-class, man, rather I *perform* my middle agedness, my whiteness, my middle classness, my masculinity, through my use of language, alongside my clothes, grooming, and general behaviour. My way of speaking helps create a particular character, and if I didn't like the character it was creating, I would probably do something to change it.

Think of a famous person who is known to have a distinctive, even iconic, accent. Is that accent simply the inevitable result of their upbringing and social background? Or is it being used, emphasised, and exaggerated in order to help create and maintain a particular professional persona? I'm thinking about people such as Russell Brand, Chris Rock, Christopher

Walken, Danny Dyer, Ray Winstone, Dolly Parton, Cilla Black, Matthew McConaughey, Chris Eubank, Fran Drescher. For these people and many others, their accent is (or was), arguably, a big part of who they are professionally. This isn't a bad thing at all, and neither is it inauthentic. In fact, not knowing any of these people personally, I can't be completely sure they don't speak in exactly the same way when they are at home as they do when they are in front of the TV cameras.[4] Let's just call it a professional hunch. Maybe you have your own distinctive professional persona that requires a conscious change in the way you speak, and when you come home you simply change out of it along with your work clothes. Unless it's a change that you feel pressured to adopt unwillingly (or have even been forced to adopt), it's not necessarily a bad thing. It's just the way we operate as humans.

Linguists Robert Le Page and Andrée Tabouret-Keller would see the linguistic choices we make as constituting 'acts of identity' — ways of aligning ourselves with particular groups of people, or with particular identities.[5] Is this conscious or unconscious? It probably depends on the situation. But it's usually true that we do have some agency when it comes to how we present ourselves, and how we are perceived by others, in our day-to-day lives — and how we speak, and how we adapt our speech in different situations, is one of the most fundamental ways we do this.

You say tomato

Before we go any further, it is worth pausing to consider what we actually mean when we refer to the way we speak and the ways in which we adapt this speech. Language, especially spoken language, is inherently variable. It is available to be used in different ways, at different times, for different purposes.

Of course, there is the obvious variation between identifiably different languages, such as English, Spanish, and Urdu, but there is also variation within the same language, or between different dialects. Spoken language varies between speakers: you speak differently from your friend. It varies between groups of speakers: you and your friends from your local area are likely to speak differently from a group of people from another area. And it even varies within an individual because as we have already seen, you change the way you speak from one context to another.

Just to complicate things even more, this variation can happen at different 'levels' of language. It can happen at the level of individual words, or what we call 'lexis': for example, let's look at all the different ways of referring to a bread roll in the UK — you might call it a bap, a barm, a muffin, a cob, or a bun, or something else entirely, depending on where you are from, and possibly even how old you are. It might occur at a sentence level, in how you structure what you are saying: for example, you might use features of African American English (AAE) such as 'habitual be', where 'she be driving' means she often, or habitually drives, rather than necessarily indicating she is driving right now.

Then there is, of course, huge variation in how we pronounce individual words, or what linguists call 'phonology'. For example, does the word *dance* have the same vowel sound as *Dan* or *darn*? Do the words *paw, poor,* and *pour* all sound the same, or do they all sound different? What about the words *Mary, merry,* and *marry*?

These differences in pronunciation are in their own special sub-category of dialect — *accent* — which refers only to the sounds of speech, and not the words and grammar. While all variation is interesting, accent is perhaps especially interesting, as this is where most variation takes place. When we consider lexical variation, we are only looking at those instances where a particular word comes up. (How many conversations actually include a discussion of bread rolls, or sports shoes, or small alleyways between houses?) But when we consider phonological variation, we are looking at every single time a particular sound is uttered, whatever the word. The sound 'th' and all the different ways it can be pronounced appears a lot more frequently in everyday speech than however you ask for a cheese roll.

Say 'Ahhhh'

I'm using quite a broad definition of accent here, one that is common within linguistics, the academic discipline that studies language, but perhaps less common in general usage, where discussions about accents tend to be tied very closely to particular sounds, such as the 'a' sound in *dance* mentioned above, and their relation to geographical regions or social class. Throughout this book, you can assume that I'm taking accent to include any sound used in speech. To get you started with thinking about this, here are a few of the most important ones:

Differences in vowel sounds, such as those in *bath*, *bus*, and *face*, are responsible for a great deal of variation in spoken language. Based on how someone in England pronounces *bath*, *past*, or *mast*, we can locate their likely regional background as being either 'southern' or 'midlands/northern'. Likewise, if British ears hear the word *lot* pronounced something like 'laht', then they are likely to assume it is coming from an American speaker.

Notice that I'm referring to 'vowel sounds' (and 'consonant sounds') rather than simply 'vowels' and 'consonants'. This is to avoid confusion with letters of the alphabet and issues of spelling. In the Modern English alphabet there are 21 consonants and five vowels, but in speech there are many more sounds than this. Think, for example, of the different vowel sounds produced by the single vowel letter 'o' in words such as *tomb, work, women, wok, wolf,* and *won*.

We usually think of English as having around 44 sounds, but it depends on the accent. Some English accents from the north of England have the same vowel sound for the words *put* and *putt*, so they might have one less sound overall than people from the south. However, they might also have a long 'eh' sound in words like *face*, which gives them a vowel sound not found in the south.

There are also extra sounds such as the glottal stop, which is made when the airflow is stopped and then released by the vocal folds. Think of the sound that exists between the two parts of 'Uh-ho!' — that's a glottal stop. Glottal stops don't alter the meaning of words in English (although they can in other languages), but they do contribute to the overall accent.

Consonant sounds are generally less variable than vowel sounds, but they do still create important differences in pronunciation. Consider the 't' sound in the word *butter*. This can be pronounced as a clear 't' (think of a BBC news reader), as something like 'd' (think of a US accent), or as a glottal stop (think of a traditional London cockney accent). Similarly, the 'ing' in *sleeping* can be pronounced as 'ing', as 'in', or even as 'inG', where the 'g' is pronounced in the same way as it would be in a word such as *give*. The first two pronunciations are common in many varieties of English, but the third one is only found in some parts of the UK, such as the north-west of England. For speakers who have this third pronunciation, the words *finger* and *singer* will rhyme.

Variation can also occur in the pitch movement of the voice, what we call intonation. Some accents or particular voices are considered quite monotone. The UK's Birmingham accent is often perceived in this way, as is the New Zealand accent — although perhaps not by people from Birmingham or New Zealand themselves. Other accents show a great deal of variation. One intonation pattern that is often commented upon is when someone's voice pitch rises at the end of a statement. Known technically as 'uptalk' or 'high-rising terminal', this is a speech phenomenon that is often associated with young, particularly American, women, although you'll hear it in the UK too, and it is extremely common in Australia (in fact, you might see it referred to as Australian Questioning Intonation).

There was a theory that uptalk came to the UK in the 1980s via the Australian soap opera *Neighbours*, as it sounded particularly Australian to British ears, but this has generally been discredited.[6] I mean, it would be great if it were true — that if every time a TV programme became popular it would generate a change in accent across sections of society. I'd be especially impressed by those who would now be speaking like the Peaky Blinders! A lot of people are convinced that it does actually happen, and will evidence it by describing how their kids will watch various TV programmes and suddenly sound American/British/Australian. Honestly, from a linguistic perspective, any such effect is generally very slight and very temporary. It makes sense that young children might imitate characters from the shows they watch, and it could even be the case that a slight pronunciation difference hangs around for a while, but family and friends have a far greater influence on the speech of children than TV longer term.[7]

As well as individual sounds and intonations, variation in pronunciation can happen in terms of voice quality — whether a voice is perceived as smooth, gravelly, rich, or thin, for example. Or whether it demonstrates what's known as 'creaky voice'. Creaky voice or 'vocal fry' is another speech feature that is often associated with young, especially American, women. Combined with uptalk, it provides the toolkit for what is often referred to as 'Valley Girl' speech, and is a feature that is often heavily stigmatised. In 2015, the author and journalist Naomi Wolf described her own antipathy towards what she sees as this 'destructive speech pattern'.[8]

We will discuss vocal fry more in Chapter 3, but for a quick example of what it actually sounds like, go and listen to a recording of the US media personality Kim Kardashian or the actor Zooey Deschanel. I could also suggest you listen to a recording of Bradley Cooper discussing his film *A Star is Born*, but that would give away a crucial point I will make later about gender stereotypes and language. (Spoiler: he uses vocal fry a LOT, yet unlike his female counterparts he doesn't get called unintelligent or an airhead as a result. Interesting.)

Start listening!

I urge you to spend some time thinking about your voice the next time you are out and about and interacting with people. See if you can identify how and when your voice, accent, or speech style changes, or think about how your voice might be perceived by others. If, even then, you're still convinced that the way you speak doesn't change, listen to people around you. Really listen. Not just to what they say, but to how they say it.

(I should warn you, though, that when you start doing this, you run the risk of missing what people say when they are talking to you, as you are focusing on the 'wrong' thing. Many's the time my wife has pulled me up on this. It turns out I have a particular facial expression that indicates when I've stopped listening to the content of what she's saying and am thinking about her accent instead. Apparently, I even start quietly recreating the particular interesting sound to myself as she's still speaking. At this point she rolls her eyes and says, 'Okay, what have I said that sounds funny?' I try not to do this anymore. I think it's for the best.)

So why does our speech vary so much? Why are there so many different ways of pronouncing the same words? The next chapter explores this variety of accents by doing a bit of digging into the past.

CHAPTER 1

Why are there so many accents?

When we notice different 'regional' accents, wherever we live in the world and whatever language we speak, we are getting not just an insight into the present, but a glimpse into the past. How we talk is often the result of complex histories of invasion, settlement, war, alliance, power, economics, mobility, friendship, and hostility. Oh, and a bit of linguistic mystery. But before we start unravelling some of the threads that make up the tapestry of the English language and its global varieties, it is worth remembering two things. Firstly, language is incredibly fluid and malleable, and it is constantly changing. This cannot be overstated — all languages evolve, all the time. English now is not the same as English in Shakespeare's time. English now is not even the same as English in your grandparents' time. In fact, if we're being really picky, English now isn't the same as English yesterday. Someone, somewhere, is right now using a new word; or is using an old word in a slightly new way; or is pronouncing a sound just a little bit differently from their friends; or is being creative with their grammar. And while some of these innovations will disappear as quickly as they appeared, others will stick around and be used and adapted by other speakers. Secondly, language change does not happen by itself — it is people who change language. It is people who are influenced by various social, political, and cultural factors throughout their lives, and it is people who then use language to make sense of their world. Language is often viewed as a living entity, but without people to use it, it would stagnate and die.

It is also people who write history, choosing what to include and what to omit, shaping our narratives with their own biases and agendas. Before we delve into our linguistic past, we need to be aware that what follows is simply one story of how the English language got to be how it is today. Most documented histories of 'English' are really histories of the version of English known as 'Standard English' (which, despite never having been the language that is most frequently used in our everyday lives, is still a useful way in).[1] So, here is the story of how Standard English evolved in the British Isles, which is just the starting point of many other stories, told and untold, about how the English language went on to develop around the world.

The earliest spoken 'English'

Where did it all begin? The furthest back we can go with any kind of certainty is around 449 AD, when, according to Bede, a monk and historian born in the 7th century, Britain — then made up of several tribes speaking various Celtic languages unrelated to modern-day English — began to be invaded by significant numbers of Germanic Jutes, Angles, and Saxons from modern-day Germany, Denmark, and the Netherlands. We say 'invaded', but remember Bede's account was written several hundred years after the fact, when things might have been remembered as being slightly more dramatic than they actually were. The chances are that there was already considerable contact between the Britons and people from continental Europe through trading, so these 'invaders' weren't exactly previously unknown enemies appearing from nowhere. Most likely, the process was more one of 'settlement, acculturation and accommodation' over a period of time.[2] Similar to the Britons, these incomers were not homogenous in their culture and language, even within their own regional groups.

Before all this happened, the various local Celtic languages in Britain had probably existed in some form since the arrival of people from mainland Europe in the Bronze and Iron Ages. The Romans had then moved in from 43 to 410 AD, so there was some Latin influence too, although less than you might think, as there wasn't a great deal of mixing between the occupiers and the Indigenous peoples. Then, when the Saxons and their friends arrived, the Britons — who already had a mixed linguistic history — were faced with a whole new set of languages that they began to use alongside their Celtic varieties. It was these Germanic languages which would go on to become the basis of Old English. The word *English* actually comes to us via the name of one of those original groups — the Angles.

The incoming languages pushed the Celtic varieties westward, where they remained strong throughout Scotland, Ireland, Wales, Devon, Cornwall, and Cumbria, and in time developed into Scots Gaelic, Irish, Welsh, Cornish, and Breton (across the sea in Brittany). All of these languages are still used today, with some having been consciously revived and reinvigorated. But for the rest of the island, Old English, in its various versions, was beginning to dominate. For the next hundred years, the new arrivals made themselves at home. And of course, as the people spread, so did their language.

The gradual dominance and political strength of these newcomers is the likely reason behind most people adopting the new languages (in various dialects). In a sad pattern we shall see repeated again and again — if you want to access the best opportunities, the first step is to speak in a similar way to those who hold the power, even if it means virtually abandoning your own voice.

> We can still hear influences from this period in the 'regional' accents present in Britain now. For example, the reason that your friend from Scotland or the northeast of England might pronounce *house* as 'hoose' and *long* as 'lang' can be traced back to the dominance of the Angles, originally from southern Denmark, in the old Kingdom of Northumbria in the 7th and 8th centuries. Indeed, *hus* and *lang* are still the words for *house* and *long* in Danish today.

A linguistic Smörgåsbord

The next big influence on the English language came in the formidable shape of the Vikings, who started arriving in Britain in the late 8th century, and eventually took control of much of the north and east of England and the west of Scotland, leaving the Anglo-Saxons with the south and west of England. This essentially split the country into two, under an agreement known as the Danelaw, with the Vikings speaking Old Norse, and the Anglo-Saxons speaking Old English. This inevitably led to more language differences across the country, with people using language to demonstrate allegiance with a particular group.

> The influence of Old Norse on English can be seen in some of the words we use today. *Slaughter, awkward, sky, skill,* and *skirt,* among, others all originate from Old Norse. The 'sk' spelling can actually be a good clue in this direction. While many of the words exist in Standard English today, some are limited to the dialects of particular regions. For example, *skriking* meaning 'crying', can be heard in areas of the north of England.

Things carried on like this for a while until the next big invasion, this time from the Normans, led by William of Normandy, soon to be William the Conqueror, in 1066, who defeated both the Anglo-Saxon and the Viking forces. William and his people brought with them the language of Norman French, which (adapted into Anglo-Norman French) soon became the default language of power, alongside Latin, which was still the language of the church and high learning. English (which was seen as an uncultivated language) continued to exist, mainly among the general population, thus creating what is known as a triglossic situation, where three different languages serve different status-related purposes. However, by the end of the 12th century, as the Normans and the English began to intermarry, English (now with some clear French and Latin influences) made a comeback, even among higher-status people. Now it was in the form of what we know as Middle English.

> Norman French had a big influence on English, providing thousands of new words, along with prefixes (the bit that goes onto the beginning of a word such

as 'pre-' and 'en-'), and suffixes (the bit that goes onto the end of a word such as '-ment' and '-able'). A well-noted example of this influence is in the words we use for animals and the meat we get from them, where the words for animals such as *swine*, *cow*, and *sheep* come from Old English, but the words for the meat *pork*, *beef*, and *mutton* come from French.

If we take a step back for a moment, we can see that, by 1300, the inhabitants of these small islands had been exposed to (and often ruled in) Celtic varieties, Latin, Germanic varieties, Old Norse, Old English, Norman French, Anglo-Norman French, and Middle English, with Cornish still thriving in the southwest (albeit in a decreasing area), and Welsh still going strong in Wales. On top of this, very little was written down, so there was no standard variety of any of these languages. There would have been significant differences in how people spoke across the country due to varying strengths of influence of different groups in different areas and minimal travel between regions, meaning that each version of the 'English' language was free to develop in its own way.

Around this time in Scotland, Old English had been developing in a different way, into what would later become known as Scots. This language became dominant in Scotland, to the point where it was used in all official documents, as well as in literature and poetry.[3] The more it was used, the more it diverged from English, a process fuelled by ongoing animosity and conflict between the two countries. Ireland, meanwhile, had its own Celtic language, which by this point had developed into Early Modern Irish through stages now recognised as Primitive, Old, and Middle.

Over the next 200 years, far more written documents were produced, allowing us a glimpse into all this linguistic variation. Remember that in the absence of any standard rules or conventions, anybody who wrote anything down, in whatever form (records, poetry, religious texts), would have been attempting to replicate the sounds of spoken language (specifically *their* spoken language) through their choice of spelling. This means that variations and idiosyncrasies between and even within texts provide insights into the likely pronunciation patterns of the day. It is also worth remembering that at this point in time there was no real sense of any one version being better or more correct than any other; people were free to speak and write in whatever way they saw fit. Obviously, people developed preferences for this or that variety over another, but there was no reason to think one of them was superior.

That vowel is so last year

As we have seen, most of the linguistic development of Middle English can be traced through the history of who arrived in Britain at what time bringing what languages, but in the 15th and 16th centuries, an intriguing development took place, with uncertain origin (that linguistic mystery I referred to earlier). The vowel sounds people were using started to change, and this process became known as the Great Vowel Shift.

To give an example of the process, at the time, in Britain, the 'i' in words such as *bite*, *life*, or *hide* would have been pronounced the same as the 'ee' in *sheep* today, but gradually, people started to pronounce this vowel sound more like we do now, perhaps as they came into contact with other people, perhaps due to influence from French. And then something extraordinary happened — as this vowel shifted, others then also had to shift in order to remain different from one another. Words such as *meet* and *deep*, which would then have been pronounced with an elongated 'e' sound (think of the word *set* but hold the vowel sound to make it longer), started being pronounced with the 'ee' sound we recognise today (and which was vacated by the 'i' sound in words like *bite*). And then, as this group of words changed, it started to leave another space into which another vowel sound moved, and so on.

It is worth emphasising the slowness and duration of the change — it's not simply the case that everybody woke up with a whole new vowel system one day (which would be both odd and hilarious), neither was it a conscious decision by a group of people to start pronouncing particular words differently. At any one point in time, people of different ages and different backgrounds would have been using slightly different pronunciations, but all these differences were contributing to an underlying systematic change in the vowel system of English over a few hundred years.

> Now, I know that the following diagram is going to be unfamiliar to some readers, but bear with me. It's basically a representation of the 'position' of vowels. Or, more accurately the position of the tongue when producing those vowels. Before you have a proper look, think about what's going on in your mouth when you produce the word, *please*. In fact, say the word, but really elongate the vowel sound in the middle, and over-pronounce as though you are about to go on stage and this is your vocal warm up. You should notice that your tongue is quite high, towards the roof of your mouth. You can test this by now moving from saying *please* to saying *cat*, when your mouth will open to allow your

tongue to go lower, away from the roof of your mouth. The vowel in *please* is therefore known as a 'high' or 'close' vowel, and the vowel in *cat* is known as a 'low' or 'open' vowel. Now go back to saying *please*, but this time change to saying *took* and pause when you are saying the vowel. Again, really emphasise the pronunciation. You should notice two things — firstly that your lips are now rounded, but also, that your tongue has moved backwards in your mouth. You can try alternating between *please* and *took* to really feel the movement. The vowel in *took* is known as a 'back' vowel, while the vowel in *please* is a front vowel.

We can then visualise these vowel positions on a vowel chart, which is basically an abstract representation of the mouth, looked at side-on with the person facing to the left. So, the vowels in *please*, *cat*, and *took* would look like this:

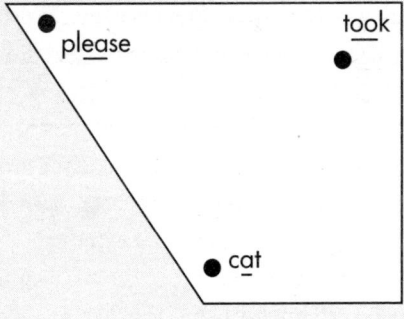

If we then use a similar diagram to illustrate the changes in the great vowel shift, it would look something like the diagram below. I've added the phonetic symbols for those readers who are familiar with them, but for everyone else, I will try to explain. The easiest way to think about it is to start with the word *name* but use an 'ah' sound for the 'a'. Then each stage of the shift up the left side of the diagram is a gradual movement towards an 'ee' sound (like *please* above). Each example word is placed in its position before it shifted to the next place along the chain. Words such as *name* started with an 'ah' sound, then moved to a kind of an 'eh' sound, then moved to where it is now if you think of a BBC newsreader-like pronunciation. Interestingly, in some varieties it didn't make that final move and stayed as the 'flat' vowel we associate with northern English accents. On the other side of the diagram, it's the same story, with each vowel moving up, changing *mouth* from being pronounced as 'mooth' to where it is now. But again, this last shift didn't occur in all accents (I'm looking at you, Scotland).

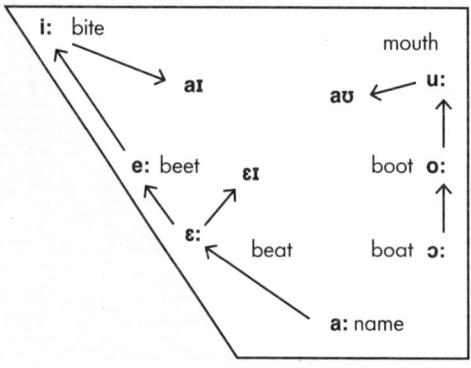

While we might not be completely sure why the changes started, we can be quite sure of how they spread, which was, obviously, through contact between people. And there was a great deal of this during this period due to significant population shifts following the Black Death (a bubonic plague pandemic that arrived in England in 1348). Rural peasants and other workers were in high demand after the loss of almost half of the population, meaning that they could move to wherever the money was better. To these new areas, they brought their own distinct dialect varieties, and in turn they were exposed to local ways of speaking that were new to them. Certain dialects began to acquire more or less social status depending on who spoke them, with some sounds undoubtedly being associated with the peasants, and others with higher society. And when this happens, what is known as 'hypercorrection' soon follows, as individual speakers try to match the vowels and other pronunciations of the people around them.

Hypercorrection describes the practice of 'overdoing' an attempt to use a 'prestigious' form of language. I'll give a relatively up-to-date example. My late grandfather grew up and lived in a part of the UK in which the word *but* has the same vowel sound as *foot*, which does not match the more 'standard' pronunciation found in the typically wealthier, more powerful south of England (more on this shortly). Having a vague awareness that there was something 'wrong', or at least 'less posh', about the way he pronounced words with a 'u' in them (not just *but*, but also *nut*, *sunny*, and *tub*), and being someone who cared about such things, he would sometimes alter his pronunciation to sound 'posher'. But in doing so, he would sometimes overcorrect himself and create an entirely new sound: asking for 'shuggar' in his tea, for example. A mistake easily recognised, laughed about, and then rectified in our modern, more standardised, world.[4]

Now, imagine my grandfather, Jim, as a rural labourer in the 16th century at the time of King Henry VIII. He has travelled to get some work from powerful people elsewhere in the country. While he's there, he's exposed to a whole different way of speaking. He can understand it, but lots of the words sound different to him. He begins to adopt some of these new pronunciations in his own speech, both to make communication with other people easier, and to avoid drawing too much attention to his outsider peasant status. After a few months, or even years of working, he returns home to his wife, Nellie, and friends, and tells them all of his experiences. Everyone comments on Jim's new accent, but Jim doesn't mind — he's proud of what he sees as a mark of esteem. He even starts exaggerating his new pronunciations to demonstrate even more strongly how he has moved up in the world. And when he comes across a word that he isn't 100 per cent sure how to pronounce in his new accent (such as *sugar*), well, he simply has a guess! And of course, all of this starts to rub off on Jim's family and friends. They look at Jim and think, 'There's a man who's going up in the world, just listen to his fancy accent!' And so they start to copy Jim's way of speaking, hypercorrections and all. Before you know it, a whole new group of people are starting to use Jim's new pronunciations, and they in turn pass them on to their own families and friends, with varying degrees of accuracy. But equally, there will be a whole other group of people who resolutely stick to their original ways of speaking as they look at Jim and think, 'Well who the hell does he think he is?'

Anyway, back to the real history. The Great Vowel Shift (which is generally seen to have been complete by around

1700, despite not all areas of the country undergoing the same degree of change) had a huge effect on the way English was pronounced. It also had an effect on our spelling system. While some spellings were changed to reflect the new pronunciations, others weren't, a situation which helped to create the inconsistent and idiosyncratic system we are left with today.

When I say that 'spellings were changed', you might wonder 'by who'? (Or possibly 'by whom?', which would put you in the middle of a language change that is happening right now: chances are, if you're under 25, you rarely, if ever, use *whom*.) Technically nobody is in charge of English spelling, even now, so nobody has the power to decide on changes. But this is precisely the point in the history of English when consistency was starting to emerge, and certain people did begin, in a sense, to put themselves in charge not only of spelling, but also grammar, and later, pronunciation. The problem is, no one really asked them to, and these people didn't necessarily know what they were doing.

It's all about London

Before the Great Vowel Shift, there had started to be some consistency in the ways in which the English language was written down. This is particularly evident in the documents that were transcribed in and around London, a city that was growing as a centre of power, and whose variety of English began to dominate, albeit with significant influence from the dialects of the wider East Midlands dialect area (this was an area much bigger than what we think of as the East Midlands now — it included Cambridge and Oxford and was more densely populated than other areas). Of special significance was the operation of the Chancery, whose dealings with legal documents demanded a certain degree of consistency. It wasn't just official writing that had begun to develop a need for standardisation, though — the increase in writing of all types encouraged a consensus of shared usage.

Then, in 1476, a man named William Caxton helped cement the status of the variety of English spoken in the south of England as 'standard' forever. Caxton set up a printing press in London's Westminster, having learned the process in Europe. This press allowed him to produce and re-produce texts far more easily than before, when everything had had to be written out by hand. Crucially, the printing press created a consistency that had been absent in written English until that point. Previously, even the most meticulous scribes would make mistakes, and would have their own ways of translating, spelling, or phrasing particular ideas, but the printing press got rid of all that variation. Well, kind of. Caxton and the people who worked with him were still individuals with their own habits and preferences. The only difference was that their idiosyncrasies were immortalised and repeated in texts that were printed multiple times.

Caxton faced a genuine issue when it came to reproducing the English language in print, which was, quite simply: which variety should he choose? Imagine the situation. Caxton has this new technology that he probably already senses has the potential to revolutionise the production of texts, and he is beyond excited to try it out and impress everyone. He sets everything up, and is all ready to start creating his first piece, when he is, straight away, faced with a question: should he spell this word like this, or like that? Should he use the version he knows from growing up in Kent, in the south of England, or the version he hears and sees in Westminster, the political district of London? The fact is, he would have been surrounded by great variety in both the spoken language around him, and in the written language created by various scribes. He had to decide which specific forms to use, and which, therefore, to unconsciously elevate to some kind of state of permanence. In many ways he was single-handedly (and slightly reluctantly) trying to standardise English, which, as we have seen, until this point, had been very much free to vary. The task was, of course, impossible, and Caxton's early work especially was full of inconsistencies as he rushed from one job to the next, relying on large numbers of typesetters who had their own preferences and idiosyncrasies. He even wrote of the problems facing him in the prologue to one of his translations. He recounted the story of a merchant who tried to buy food from a woman, but neither could understand the other's word for *eggs*, as one used 'egges' and the other used 'eyren', both English forms, but from different parts of the country. Caxton sums it up by asking, 'Lo, what sholde a man in thyse days now wryte: egges or eyren? Certaynly it is harde to playse every man because of dyversity and change of language.'[5]

Caxton was clearly aware of the different varieties of English, and of the challenges facing him in making sure his printed works were accessible to as wide a range of people as possible. This was not driven by any altruistic need to share knowledge and learning, nor was it fuelled by any particular interest in language itself or its standardisation, but simply by the need to make money. The more people who could understand his work, the more he would be able to sell. This made people who could read and had money and influence especially important to Caxton; it made commercial sense to target and even court those groups in particular. The result was an emphasis on the English found in London, and in the triangle of influence between London, Oxford, and Cambridge, the political and academic centres of England. This was the variety used by educated, literate, and influential people with money, and so this was the variety that made most commercial sense for Caxton to use.

This was a hugely important episode in the development of English because it began to formalise the idea that there is one superior form of the language. Caxton's decision to use the dialects of the rich and powerful may have been made for commercial rather than linguistic reasons, but as a result, the linguistic status of the rich and powerful was enhanced. It was their variety of English that was to now be associated with the works of Chaucer and other prestigious writers and so it was their variety of English that benefited from the second-hand glow of sophistication and authority. And the after-effects of that glow still continue to this day. Once the English of London, Oxford, and Cambridge began to be established in print as the variety of importance by Caxton, other printers followed suit. And once there was the sense of a 'better' variety of language to be used in print, that affected people's perception of how language should be spoken.

> What would have happened if the powerful people of England had lived somewhere other than the south-east of the country? Would this have changed the development of English? Imagine if somewhere a couple of battles had gone another way, a different group of people living in a different area of the country had been dominant, and York had ended up as the capital. Or Lancaster, or Lincoln, or Doncaster. It is very likely that Caxton would have ended up there, rather than in London, and he would have chosen to reproduce the dialects of the educated and influential from that area

in his printing. Just think how different things would be right now if York was the English capital. For a start, King Charles would have the best Yorkshire accent going, with people near and far wishing they could emulate his immaculate 'flat' vowels. Newspaper articles would be written about the younger royals becoming less posh by softening their Yorkshire ways of speaking in an effort to be more relatable. People who had grown up in Surrey would desperately try to shake off their tell-tale southern accents as they battled for acceptance among the great and good of the north. Southerners would be throwing their smart speakers through the window in despair at their inability to understand the simplest instructions. And people like me would be on the radio ('He's a Professor?[6] With that accent?!') arguing for a future in which the BBC might actually employ a newsreader from London, or from Berkshire, or from anywhere other than Yorkshire. But no, it was London that became the capital, so it was London and its surrounding areas that housed the people with the power, and it was their dialect that gained prestige and would eventually become the standard.

We haven't quite finished our history of British English accents and dialects yet, but hopefully you can already see the role of chance and opportunity in the story so far. So-called 'standard' English did not emerge as the result of some linguistic battle of quality and fitness for purpose, where the most effective and objectively more superior version of the language naturally filtered to the top. Rather, it emerged as the result of historical accident and business acumen. Remember that the next time someone seems to be implying that their dialect is somehow better than yours.

Actually, here's something else to remember if you have a northern English accent and somebody decides to comment on the way you say *funny* or *but*: your pronunciation was the original! Up until the 17th century, everybody pronounced the vowel sound in words like *sun* and *cut* the same as they did in words like *put* and *full*. Gradually, the pronunciation of some of these words changed in the south of England, but remained the same in the north. To this day, this difference (technically known as the FOOT/STRUT split, indicating that the original single vowel sound in these two words split to become two separate vowel sounds) is one of the key differences between northern and southern varieties of English in England. In the north, the words *put* and *putt* will sound the same or similar. In the south, they will sound different.

I prescribe some grammar

By now we are moving into what is known as Early Modern English. The printing and sharing of further influential texts continued to cement one centralised version of the language. The King James Bible of 1611 and the works of Shakespeare are some of the most well-known texts of this time, and the influence of the latter on the development of English is still widely studied and discussed.

This was also a period in which dictionaries and grammar guides started to make an appearance, notably Samuel Johnson's *A Dictionary of the English Language* in 1755.[7] Johnson's dictionary is particularly interesting as the final version appears to take a much more descriptive approach (as in, describing how the language is actually used, as opposed to a prescriptive approach which indicates how language *should* be used) than

Johnson had originally planned. In his 1747 document *The Plan of an English Dictionary*, Johnson writes, 'The chief intent of it is to preserve the purity and ascertain the meaning of our English idiom.'[8] Yet when faced with the difficulty of actually doing this in a systematic and accountable way, his approach shifted, so much so that in the preface of the dictionary itself he writes at some length about the impossibility of fixing the language in the way he had envisaged: '... may the lexicographer be derided who being able to produce no example of a nation that has preserved their words and phrases from mutability, shall imagine that his dictionary can embalm his language, and secure it from corruption and decay, that it is in his power to change sublunary nature, or clear the world at once from folly, vanity, and affectation'.[9] But even with this more descriptive approach, there is no doubt that the influence of this work led to further regularity, shaping the language we still use today.

While Johnson's dictionary showed some awareness and acceptance of the ever-changing nature of English, there were plenty of other people who had a much more rigid view. Bishop Robert Lowth's *A Short Introduction to English Grammar* (1762) is often given as an example of a book of inflexible ideas as to the rights and wrongs of English, although not entirely fairly. Prominent writers of the time such as John Dryden, Daniel Defoe, and Jonathan Swift felt that the language needed some discipline. Swift was particularly strident in his view that English needed to be 'fixed', in order to halt its needless rapid change and deterioration.[10] One interesting thing all these dictionaries and grammar guides had in common is the fact that, while they often showed sound linguistic understanding, their decisions as to what to prescribe as 'correct'(and therefore what to proscribe as 'incorrect') were based on personal preference and spurious etymological reasoning rather than linguistic evidence.

Meanwhile in Scotland, the newly standardised variety of English was starting to overpower the status of Scots, perhaps an inevitable consequence of the Union of the Crowns of England and Scotland in 1603. However, Scots did not disappear by any means. Although people seeking power and prestige clamoured to use Standard English, everyday people were quite happy, and proud, to speak as they always had. Down in Cornwall, Cornish was just about hanging on, but its days were numbered, having been pushed to the very edge of the county geographically. Irish was still going strong in Ireland, although it was soon to become a minority rather than majority language. And over in Wales, Welsh was struggling against the imposition of laws prioritising English as an administrative language and a general shift towards all things English by those at the top of Welsh society. Ominously, what was happening linguistically within Britain was soon to be replicated globally as Britain continued with its colonisation of a quarter of the globe.

After the first flurry of writings about grammar, there started to appear similar works focusing on pronunciation. Thomas Sheridan published *A General Dictionary of the English Language* in 1780 — the first serious attempt to provide a specific pronunciation of every word. This was followed by John Walker's *A Critical Pronouncing Dictionary* in 1791, which explicitly aimed to improve on Sheridan's offering, and to provide advice as to how to speak 'correctly'. And of course, you don't need me to tell you which variety of English was chosen to represent the 'correct' pronunciation of English. In fact, the preface to John Walker's work provides some fascinating insights into the way he (and presumably others) viewed the pronunciation differences across the country. At one point he suggests that 'those at a considerable distance from the capital do not only mispronounce many words taken separately, but they scarcely pronounce with purity a single word, syllable, or letter'.[11] But this doesn't mean that all Londoners were seen to be blessed with superior pronunciation. While he explicitly identifies an 'educated' or 'cultured' London accent as the best and most desirable way to speak, Walker actually saves his strongest criticism for 'vulgar' (cockney) London speech, which is 'a thousand times more offensive and disgusting' than even the erroneous speech of 'Scotland, Ireland, or any of the provinces'.[12]

Then, as now, people did not just *notice* differences in the speech of those from different areas, they also had strong feelings about those differences (remember Steph McGovern?). And in sharing those feelings, especially if the person had any position of authority on the issue (real or imagined), particular pronunciations became regarded as 'vulgar' by more people in a vicious cycle of linguistic snobbery.

Speaking proper

By the 1800s, we are into the Modern English period. The English language is well on its way across the globe via colonialism, creating even more linguistic diversity as people are forced to use the language of their oppressors in combination with, or instead of, their own languages. Back in the UK, English continues to develop and change, with a renewed sense of awareness of its broad dialectal variation.

At this time, an explosion of publications advising people on how to speak and write 'better' English had led to a much greater awareness of regional and social differences among ordinary people, with language differences now routinely, and sometimes problematically, used as a source of humour or staged misunderstanding in novels and cartoons. The work of Charles Dickens is especially rich in this regard, using written dialect and accent to indicate both regional and social-class differences between characters. For example, the dialogue of cockney Sam Weller in *The Pickwick Papers* is full of accent features, including the then common blurring of 'v' and 'w':

> 'Nev'r mind, Sammy,' replied Mr Weller, 'it'll be a wery agonisin' trial to me at my time of life, but I'm pretty tough, that's vun consolation, as the wery old turkey remarked wen the farmer said he wos afeerd he should be obliged to kill him for the London market.'[13]

And then there's Stephen Blackpool, a factory worker in *Hard Times*, whose dialect is intended to reflect the fictional Coketown, in Lancashire:

> 'My friends,' Stephen began, in the midst of a dead calm; 'I ha' hed what's been spok'n o' me, and 'tis lickly that I shan't mend it. But I'd liefer you'd hearn the truth concernin myseln, fro my lips than fro onny other man's, though I never cud'n speak afore so monny, wi'out bein moydert and muddled.'[14]

Obviously, this wouldn't happen nowadays. We've moved on from using overblown stereotypical accents in drama and comedy, haven't we?

Once we get into the 1900s, things start to become a lot more familiar, not least because we have access to audio recordings from this period of people who were born decades earlier. The British Library website has various recordings from the early 1900s, as well as one from as far back as 1890 featuring none other than Florence Nightingale, who was alive for much of the

1800s. In many of these, we begin to hear the famous clipped tones we associate with early BBC broadcasts.

This famous accent is what is called Received Pronunciation, or RP. The term was first used to classify a particular style of pronunciation by the linguist A. J. Ellis in 1869, but was popularised by Daniel Jones in the second edition of his *English Pronouncing Dictionary* in 1924. In the first edition, he referred to it as the pronunciation of 'Southern English people who have been educated at the public schools', so you can get an idea of its nature, public schools meaning privately paid-for, and usually very expensive, education in the UK.[15] The word 'received' is used here in the same sense as in 'received wisdom', meaning 'accepted' or approved', and is in many ways an extension of everything we have already discussed — the speech varieties of the elite in society being used as a model for others. And where did the elite happen to grow up, be educated, and eventually work? London and the south-east.

The status of RP was further strengthened when it became the voice of the BBC. This was a conscious choice made by what became the BBC's Committee on Spoken English in 1926, when it was decided (by a group of educated white men from the social elite) that RP (the accent spoken by educated white men from the social elite) would be the most widely understood accent both in the UK and overseas. In a fascinating interview from 1967, John Reith, the first director-general of the BBC said that the accent was chosen as it would not 'particularly irritate one part of the country, or any part', alleging the perceived regional neutrality of RP. Faced with the comment that the BBC accent 'somehow identified the BBC with a certain section of society, certain social trends, so that to this day, the BBC is thought of as the organ of, as it were, genteel and respectable elements in society', his immediate response was 'Anything wrong with that?'.[16] 'BBC Pronunciation' soon became synonymous with Received Pronunciation, strengthening the idea that there was one superior way of speaking which should act as a model for everyone else. Over the years, the role of RP at the BBC has changed, and ever since the 1960s there has been a conscious push away from the traditional RP of its early announcers and newsreaders.

RP itself has also changed, as any accent is prone to do. Very few people today speak in the same way as those early BBC announcers and newsreaders. In fact, linguists sometimes refer to there being two 'RPs' — the one that describes the actual language used by speakers at the top of the social scale, which adapts and changes like any variety does, and the one that describes an abstract idealised way of speaking that nobody really uses anymore. There is even debate as to whether we need to abandon the term 'RP' altogether. Certainly, there is a case for observing the distinction between the two by renaming the variety that is in use, and leaving RP as the label for a fossilised variety that fulfils the role of an archaic ideal. The variety that is still being used definitely needs a name, and one that has a link to its history. Recent suggestions include General British (to reflect the established term 'General American' to describe a regionless standard), or Standard Southern British English (although this lacks the regionless aspect). Neither is perfect, so perhaps we should simply stick with RP after all, or at least Modern RP. This goes some way to capture the fact that although the speech of privately educated upper-class people today is different from the speech of privately educated upper-class people from the 1900s, these people still sound different from most other people across the country. Accents change, but the social barriers that they reflect and maintain do not.

Mixing things up

So, where does this leave us now? The reason we have so many accents in the UK is, in many ways, because of the history of the people that have lived here since the very early days. But it's also due to new people arriving and adding to the linguistic mix more recently. The period after World War II saw people from former British colonies in the Caribbean come to live and work in the UK, people who would soon identify as Black British, and who would play a significant role in British culture and language over the following decades.[17] One of the hot topics of sociolinguistics in the UK over recent years has been the emergence of what's known as Multicultural London English,[18] and a possible Multicultural British English.[19] Both are ways of speaking that have at least some of their roots planted firmly in the linguistic histories of the various Black British communities.

> One accent feature that is common in Multicultural British English and which has at least some of its roots in varieties of Black British English is what's known as 'th-stopping'. This is where 'th' sounds are pronounced as 't' or 'd', so *three* becomes 'tree' and *thing* becomes 'ting'. Related to this is what's sometimes called 'dh-stopping', where *them* becomes 'dem' and *with* becomes 'wid'. Dh-stopping is a feature of Black British varieties, but it appears in other British accents too, such as in a Liverpool accent. Incidentally, if you want to know why th-stopping and dh-stopping are separate, it all has to do with our voices. The 'th' in *three* is what's known as a voiceless sound, meaning our vocal folds aren't vibrating as we say it. This is why it changes to

't', another voiceless sound. However, the 'th' in *them* is voiced, meaning our vocal folds are vibrating when we say it, and so this changes to the equally voiced 'd'. You can feel the difference between voiceless and voiced sounds by putting your fingers on your throat (outside, not inside!) and slowly saying the 'th' in *three*. You shouldn't feel anything. Now slowly say 'th' as if you are about to say *them*; now you should feel some vibration and hear your voice. This is the movement of your vocal folds. Lots of English consonants have a voiced and voiceless pair, where they are pronounced in the same way, except that one uses the voice, and one doesn't, for example 's' and 'z', 'f' and 'v' and 'ch' (as in *chin*) and 'g' (as in *gin*).

And then there is the significant British Asian (especially South Asian) influence. While outsiders might see a term such as 'South Asian' and assume some kind of homogeneity, the linguist Farhana Alam highlights the diversity in such a broadly labelled group of people.[20] British South Asians are diverse at a national level (Pakistanis, Indians, Bangladeshis), at a religious level (Muslims, Sikhs, Hindus), at a linguistic level (Urdu, Punjabi, Hindi, Bengali), and at a social level. Again, significant migration in the 1950s saw people bringing this linguistic and social diversity to Britain to interact with the linguistic and social diversity that was already here, particularly in urban areas such as London, Birmingham, Manchester, and West Yorkshire. And, just as we have seen repeated throughout history, this led to the same processes of contact between people — through friendship, animosity, acceptance, isolation, solidarity, and indifference – developing our language along the way.

One feature that is common in many British South Asian accents is when the vowel in a word like *home* is pronounced as a single, steady vowel (known as a 'monophthong') rather than as a gliding vowel that moves between two sounds (known as a 'diphthong'). To hear the difference, try saying *home* like a BBC newsreader, but slowly. You should notice your mouth being open as you start the vowel with a kind of 'uh' sound, and then it closes slightly and your lips become rounded as you make the 'oh' or 'ow' sound. Now say it again, but this time use a steady 'o' sound as if you were saying the vowel in 'got' but making it longer. Of course, this second pronunciation overlaps with a lot of other English accents from England too, especially in the north of the country.

English in the UK is particularly diverse because of its history. The longer the existence of a language in a particular place, the greater diversity there will be. We only need to look at some other English-speaking countries for evidence of this. For example, there are far more regional accents in the UK and the US than there are in Australia, largely because English has had a lot more time to develop in those places, with a lot of this development happening before the days of mass communication and media.

Further afield

American English is especially fascinating, as it demonstrates how language can develop in different ways from the same source. When British settlers started setting up home in what is now known as North America, uninvited, in the 1600s, they of course brought with them their own ways of speaking, which would have reflected the particular accent and dialect of where they had grown up. Remember, this was the time of Shakespeare, before the first dictionaries, and before RP. This is important, as the timing partially accounts for a very well-known difference between most English English (as opposed to British English) accents and most American English accents today. In the 1600s, pretty much everybody in Britain would have pronounced the 'r' in words like *arm* or *far* (remember, spelling is a representation of speech, so for the 'r' to be there in the spelling, it must have at some point served a purpose). This means that all the people setting off for the colonies would have taken this pronunciation with them. But then things started to change in England, and the 'r' started not to be pronounced, except when it came before a vowel (for example, in *around*, but not in *cart*). This change seems to have started in the south-east of England, and spread from there, resulting in a situation today where the vast majority of accents in England do not pronounce the 'r', but most Scottish accents, and a few English accents in the north-west and the south-west of England still do. But in the lands that came to be the United States, the pronunciation did not change, and so 'r' in *arm* continued to be used, as it does to this day in most American accents. This feature actually has a name: 'rhoticity', and an accent that pronounces the 'r' is known as a 'rhotic' accent (the vowel in rhotic is usually pronounced like *goat* rather than *got*, otherwise it would sound a bit like an 'erotic' accent, which is a different thing altogether).

These original colonisers of North America were then followed by other groups, who came from different parts of Britain with different accents and dialects. Some found new places to be unwelcome guests, while others made contact with those who had already settled. Soon, people from other countries were trying their luck in this exciting new place, bringing different languages into the mix. And throughout all this, there was at least some contact with the Indigenous languages that were already there. Before long, there would be a whole new mix of accents, dialects, languages, cultures, and people; sometimes friendly, sometimes not: a situation ripe for linguistic adaptation and change. And, crucially, a situation away from all the specifically English influences of standardisation.

As more and more people arrived in the colonies, and as new generations were born, people's connection to any kind of Standard English from England grew less and less strong. As a result, American English and English spoken in the UK developed and changed in different ways to each other. Eventually, editor, author, and lexicographer Noah Webster, who argued that America should have its own way of speaking and writing that did not rely on looking back at Britain for some kind of standard, published his *American Dictionary of the English Language* in 1828. In contrast to Johnson's dictionary, this contained specifically American examples of words and spellings. Ever since that time, there has been a mixed and complex relationship between the two Englishes. Just as some people welcomed Webster's attempts to separate the two, others felt strongly that they should retain a more British way of speaking and writing, further fuelling the development of different ways of speaking among different groups of people.[21]

The result of all this is a large country with lots of people speaking English in different ways. Just as a Liverpool, a Glasgow, and a Swansea accent each sound completely different from one another (at least to British ears), so too do a Brooklyn, a Los Angeles, and a Nashville accent (at least to American ears). And then when you add race and ethnicity to the mix as well as just region, you get an incredible amount of linguistic diversity.[22]

We can contrast this with the story of the English language in Australia. In some ways the situation was similar to that in North America — groups of people from England setting up home (albeit not especially willingly at first) in a different country, taking land that was not theirs to take. But the difference is that settlers arrived in what they would soon name Australia much more recently, in 1788. The first group mainly comprised a mixture from south-east England (predominantly London), Ireland, and Scotland, and it is likely these accents merged to become something homogenous, yet closer to London English than the other varieties. This would have been the basis of the Australian accent we know today, especially when it became the default way of speaking for the first generations of children. The linguist Kate Burridge has written about the history of Australian English, and she puts its continued homogeneity in part down to surprisingly high population mobility in the early days, with the new variety spreading and establishing itself in various places relatively quickly.[23]

But while the accent might lack the same degree of regional variation as you'd find elsewhere, there was (and is) still social variation between groups of people from different social classes and racial backgrounds. These days, the varieties that are most likely to be identified are Standard Australian English (a category previously labelled as 'general'), Aboriginal English (comprising a wide range of sub-varieties ranging from those that are very similar to standard Australian English to those that are closer to a language known as Kriol used in the Northern Territory of Australia),[24] and Ethnocultural Australian English Varieties (combining Standard Australian English with features from other languages used by people who have migrated to Australia). And by their very nature, these three broad categories are going to include a lot of variation within them. Aboriginal English, for example, represents a number of overlapping varieties that emerged and developed as a result of contact between the estimated 250 distinct Indigenous languages and English. These varieties are complex and systematic in the same way as any other variety of English.[25]

The end of the road for accents?

Here in Britain, we are no longer routinely invaded by our European neighbours. We are now able to travel and communicate with people right across the country and the rest of the world, and we are all exposed to similar influences in the form of TV, film, radio, and music. So, what does that mean for our linguistic diversity?

Some people would have you believe that accents and dialects are dying out. In fact, only recently I saw a news story with the headline: 'northern accents could be dead in 45 years'.[26] But people have been saying that for a long time. It is true that, as older generations die, they often take with them particular bits of dialect or pronunciations that younger generations don't use (RIP 'thee, thou, and whom'). It is also true that there is a lot more similarity in the way we all speak now than there was 100 years ago. But a young person in Liverpool today still sounds different from a young person in Birmingham, or Glasgow, or the town of Ramsbottom. As does a young person in New York sound different from a young person in Reno, or Sioux Falls. So, if accents and dialects are disappearing, why hasn't it happened yet, and when will it happen?

It would be monumentally foolish to try to predict how language will change with any degree of certainty. But whatever the future holds for regional accents specifically, there will continue to be differences between the way people, and groups of people, speak. And the key reason is the topic of this book: the relationship between how we speak and who we are. The way we speak is one way in which we are able to subtly and not so subtly say, 'I belong to this group, and do not belong to that group' and also, 'you don't belong to this group'.[27] 'I align myself with this set of attitudes and behaviours and not with that set of attitudes and behaviours.' 'I am me, and I am not one of you.' And the need to express this will not change.[28] The next chapter explores this in more detail, looking at precisely how the various relationships work.

CHAPTER 2

Why we are what we speak

Think about the last time you met someone new. Actually, think about the last time you *heard* someone new. Maybe it was on the radio. What did you make of them? Did their voice surprise you in any way? Perhaps they were being interviewed because of their job, only they didn't sound the way you assumed they would — a farmer who sounded like an accountant, or a teacher who sounded like a member of the royal family. A new presenter on Radio 4 who sounded like they should be on Radio 1.[1] Even better, think about the last time you heard someone's voice, perhaps on the phone, and then went on to meet them in real life. Did the person in front of you match the initial impression you made of them based on the way they sounded?

There is a strong link between how we speak and who we are (or rather, how we *perform* who we are). But what aspects of our identities are particularly related to accent? It can't be everything. We can't tell, for example, that Serena Williams is an excellent tennis player by listening to her speak, neither can we tell that Brian from Accounts is a crook who's been embezzling company funds. But we can make some good guesses as to certain other characteristics of both Serena and Brian. The main aspects of our lives that often have a connection to our accent are the country or region where we grew up, where we live, our social background, our education, our gender, our ethnicity, and even our sexual identity. All of these are social factors that can have some relationship to the way we speak. This is not for a second to say that, on hearing somebody's voice for the first time, all of these parts of them will become apparent. And some aspects clearly have a much stronger relationship to the way we speak than others; everybody's lived experiences are different and those experiences combine to different effect, including on how we speak. This chapter will explore the relationship between these social factors and our speech, showing that in many ways, we really are what we speak. We'll start with the big ones — where we're from geographically and where we're from in terms of our social background (big because they are so relevant to speech and so much has been written about them), and then we'll look at each of the others in turn.

Regionally speaking

The places where we grow up and live clearly contribute to the way we speak, whether we are from the Welsh valleys or America's Deep South. And for many people, this is where the discussion of accent begins and ends — we tend to sound like where we are from. Because without conscious intervention — or if, for some reason, we have limited contact with people from our surrounding area — this is an almost inevitable outcome. (Of course, if we move around a lot in childhood, the effect will be mixed, but there will still be an effect.) And this influence of geography is more relevant on a local or regional level than on a national level, simply because regional accent variation is what we are most likely to encounter day to day. We are more likely to be aware of sounding Liverpudlian than of sounding British, for example. As a result, there can be a real sense of regional pride associated with our accent, or possibly a sense of embarrassment.

Our speech is initially influenced primarily by our parents or caregivers, although this soon switches to our peers in childhood. Anybody who has brought up young children in a situation where the accent at home is different from the accent of the local area will recognise this switch. I first noticed it when my eldest daughter went to nursery school. I spent a lot of time at home with her during her early years, and despite living in Bolton, an area of England where *bath* most definitely rhymes with *math*, she had something closer to my south-east England 'barth' (but without the 'r' for you rhotic speakers who always pronounce your 'r's). But when she started mixing with children and teachers from the surrounding area, her pronunciation changed to the more local version within weeks. 'Barth' became 'bath', and 'grarse' became 'grass' (rhyming with 'mass'). Incidentally, the same didn't really happen with my two other children, as both of them had older sisters with local vowels to emulate, so their accents naturally developed in a different way.

When my children were seven, 12, and 14, I thought it would be a great idea to move them from Bolton, where we lived, to Hertfordshire, where I'm from, just to see what would happen to their accents. They were at such good ages from an experimental point of view, as they were likely to have different degrees of influence from their relative peer groups and be at different stages when it came to their sense of identity. My guess was that the 14-year-old would keep her Bolton or at least a more general northern England accent, and she would do so at least partly consciously, being at an age where she had a strong sense of who she was and where she was from. The 12-year-old would gradually change to the local accent and likely all but lose the Bolton vowels, and the seven-year-old would change quickly and lose all trace of his early years. Sadly, when I ran this idea past my wife, I was told that wanting to find out what would happen to our children's accents if we moved down south was 'not a good enough reason' to leave our jobs, find a new place to live, and change their schools. So, if you're disappointed this book doesn't have a chapter describing the outcome of such a brilliant experiment, you can blame her.

> If you want to know when children start to notice different accents, it's apparently as early as five months. That's when they've been found to show a preference for a familiar local accent. By 12–19 months, they can recognise the same words across different accents. This is an important and interesting development, as it means a child is able to recognise a northern English pronunciation of *mummy* (with the first vowel sounding a bit more like the vowel in *foot*) and a southern English pronunciation (which to northern ears can sound a bit more like *'mammy'*) as referring to the same person, or that a British 'dog' and an American 'dahg' are the same animal. By the age of two, children can show accent-specific pronunciations, so will start to use a particular version of *mummy* or *dog*.[2]

But we do have some control over our accent. If you are someone who has moved away from where you grew up and feel that you have lost most of the local accent features, you will very likely have experienced slipping back into the local way of speaking when you visit friends and family, or even when you speak to them on the phone. This may seem to happen unintentionally, but the fact that you are aware of it happening suggests some degree of intent. And why shouldn't there be? After all, it is an entirely natural way to demonstrate that you belong to, or associate with, a particular group of people. More than this, it is a way of subtly, or not so subtly, reasserting your geographic or regional identity. For many people, where they come from is a big part of who they are. For some, being from Liverpool, or Dublin, or Johannesburg, or Delhi is a matter of fierce personal pride. Others feel a more passive sense of belonging to or identifying with particular geographical groupings. But however active or passive the link between an individual and a particular place, it does exist, and can be demonstrated by the way we speak.

Arabic with a Texan accent

When it comes to national, rather than regional, influences on the way we speak English, then of course someone's first language(s) come into play. If that first language happens to be English (American English, Australian English, Jamaican English, etc.), then the experience will be similar to that of different regional accents. But when someone's first language isn't English, things take a slightly different turn.

To understand this difference, we need to go back and think about how we first acquire our spoken language. As babies, we are surrounded by speech sounds. Our brain organises these sounds into a kind of system, helping us learn that this sound is different to that sound, and that when we hear them, or say them, different things happen. These systems, or sets of sounds, differ between languages, and to a lesser extent between accents of the same language. And although we have the potential to acquire any system, we restrict ourselves to the ones that we come into contact with as children. Once these sound systems have been established, particularly when the speaker has grown up in a monolingual context, it becomes the default system for all future language learning. So, an American learning Arabic will approach the task with their American sounds (actually, with their Texan, Californian, Philadelphian, etc. sounds), and an Italian learning English will make use of their Italian sounds (actually, their Tuscan, Romanesco, Milanese, etc. sounds). Now, where two sound systems (Californian American and Arabic, or Tuscan and English) overlap, there will be no noticeable difference in pronunciation of shared sounds. For example, both American English and Arabic have a vowel that sounds like the 'ee' in *sheep*, so a speaker can simply use the sound they already have from their existing language when they are speaking the new language. But where there are differences, things can be a bit trickier. If the new language has a sound that the first language doesn't have, then speakers have to learn a whole new sound, often for the first time since they were children. This is where noticeable accent features will emerge, at the places where new sounds are either acquired or not.

> For example, lots of languages (German, Mandarin, Farsi, etc.) don't have the 'th' sound we find in English *think*, and so it gets replaced with 't' or 's'. Similarly, English doesn't have the Welsh 'll' sound (in *Llanelli* for example), and most languages don't have the click sounds found in Zulu and Xhosa.

There is some research to suggest that it's not always the completely new sounds that cause the most difficulty, but rather the sounds that are nearly the same. The thinking is that we interpret those nearly-the-same sounds as being pretty much identical to ones we already have, and so we just use those instead. For example, the English vowel sound in *trap* doesn't exist in Turkish, but is quite close to another Turkish vowel sound — one found in the English word *dress*. As a result, Turkish speakers might pronounce the English word *bad* sounding more like 'bed'.

This is not to say that people can't learn to speak different languages without showing any influence from their first language (although it is far easier for children to do than adults), but the decision to do so is not entirely neutral. Mastering the pronunciation of another language to the extent that you sound like you grew up with that language requires a particular amount of effort, skill, and attention, and you have to ask yourself if it is actually desirable. Do you *want* to sound as though you are from somewhere else? And if so, why?

I look up to him, but I look down on him

There is a famous sketch from the British satirical comedy TV show *The Frost Report*, released in 1966, in which John Cleese (very tall, dressed in a suit and bowler hat, and speaking with a 'posh' English accent) looks down on Ronnie Barker (medium height, dressed in a less formal suit and trilby hat, and speaking with a less 'posh' accent), who in turn looks down on Ronnie Corbett (small, dressed in scruffy clothes and a flat cap, and speaking in a much more colloquial accent). The sketch is about the English class system, with Cleese representing the upper class, Barker the middle class, and Corbett the working class. Throughout the sketch, the order of who looks up to whom and who looks down on whom changes, although Corbett ultimately remains at the bottom.

Visually, the joke relies on the three men's height differences and the way they are dressed. Linguistically, the joke is communicated not only by what each man actually says but also by the accent of each character. Each character is given an accent that represents his social status in a way that is implicitly understood by the intended audience, much like in the examples of Dickens mentioned earlier where characters were given specific dialects as a way of positioning them socially. The joke also relies on people being familiar with both the British class system and British accents — without that familiarity it is simply three men sounding British. It reminds me of a diagram, popularised by the sociolinguist Peter Trudgill and used in sociolinguistics classes everywhere, to describe the relationship between regional accent and social status in the UK:

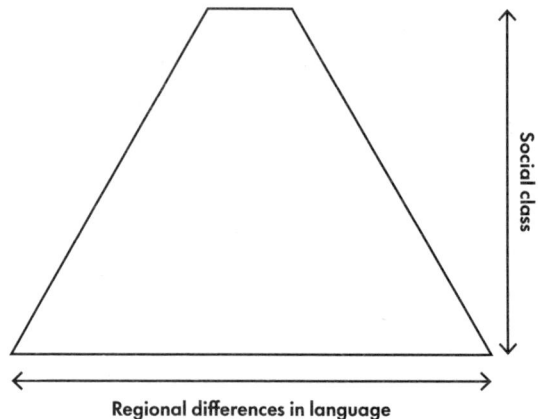

Regional differences in language

This diagram shows us that the lower down the social scale we go, the more regional variation there is; conversely, the higher up the scale we go, the less variation there is. In other words, in Britain, posh people all sound very similar to one another, no matter where they are from, and not-posh people are the ones with the strongest and most varied regional accents. This is true for many languages and countries in that there is often an accent that carries more prestige than others, and it is likely to be spoken by the elite. But why?

At the top of the diagram is Received Pronunciation (RP)—the accent of prestige and power in the UK, and England especially. Once an accent becomes associated with prestige and power, it is very likely to retain that power for a considerable period of time. It therefore becomes a self-perpetuating process: particular accents are reinforced as belonging to those at the top of a social hierarchy, and so people joining those hierarchies will seek to emulate those accents in order to fit in. In this way, accent helps to maintain a deeply embedded class system in which everybody knows their place. And if they happen to forget it, somebody will be on hand to remind them where they belong, probably mocking their inability to pronounce 'quinoa' in the process. This last point is important, as language is regularly used as a way of maintaining barriers between social classes. Remember all those 18th-century grammatical and pronunciation guides from Chapter 1, full of rules as to what was deemed correct and incorrect when it came to the English language? Remember who then used these rules and guides to make money by demonstrating to people that they didn't speak English properly? It was the group who already belonged to the elite and who wanted to make sure their club remained appropriately exclusive. And social factors are of course linked to one another. It's not just social class that groups these people together at the top of the pile, it's also the fact that, by and large, they are white men from the right parts of the country.

Imagine a school playground where a group of children take control of the climbing frame (in my childhood in the 1980s this was a thing: metal climbing frames over tarmac —

what could possibly go wrong?) and won't let anyone else on. They then devise some kind of code based on saying words in a particular way, or in a particular order, creating their own little in-group way of speaking. They use this way of speaking loudly and obnoxiously between themselves to set up a classic 'us-and-them' scenario. This way of speaking then becomes a way of policing who can join their little group and have access to the climbing frame and who can't. If you can work out the arbitrary linguistic code, you are allowed to climb on, but if you can't, you are left with another climbing-free playtime. The children who now don't have access to the climbing frame might deal with this news in different ways. There will be those who desperately want to join the climbing frame gang and will do what they can to learn the rules of the code in order to be given access. Predictably, some of these individuals will be given strong hints by a friendly insider (possibly calling in a homework favour), allowing them admission to the gang with minimal effort, making the whole process rather uneven. Then there will be the group who don't want to join the gang but do want to use the climbing frame, so might reluctantly play along and have a go at deciphering the language rules. And finally, there will be the group who think the whole thing is stupid and are not going to demean themselves by going along with pointless made-up rules simply to be able to have a go on something that should be available to everyone anyway. One day, this group will probably rise up and take control of the climbing frame themselves, along with the means to produce more climbing frames, but that is taking this already dubious analogy way beyond the scope of this book.

If we think about the class system in the UK in a very simplistic way for a moment more, along the lines of the TV sketch described previously, we have an upper class that holds the majority of wealth, power, and prestige, a working class with very little wealth, power, and prestige, and a middle class in between. Now, if I'm claiming that one of the ways in which the boundaries between the classes are maintained is through use of language, with upper-class people using a particular accent and dialect that singles them out as belonging to this exclusive club, then you might ask yourself why other people don't simply emulate that way of speaking to get ahead. When people are asked to rate different accents, RP routinely scores highly on measures of status, suggesting that people who have this accent are seen as more influential, professional, and educated than people who don't. So why don't more people simply learn to use RP in order to bask in the glow of prestigious admiration? One answer lies in the fact that 'prestige' is not a unidimensional concept. Sociolinguists like to talk of two types of prestige when it comes to language — overt prestige and covert prestige.

Overt prestige is the kind of prestige we openly associate with RP and other 'standard' ways of speaking. It is the kind of prestige that helps keep certain 'standard' accents at the top of the social hierarchy — people are consciously aware of the 'proper' ways of speaking according to the norms of a given society. Covert prestige, on the other hand, is the less obvious prestige attached to more 'non-standard' ways of speaking — perhaps a way of speaking that is strongly associated with a particular region, or with a particular section of society. It attaches positive value to ways of speaking that would not be seen as prestigious by mainstream society, which is influenced by the tradition of overtly prestigious norms. Returning to the three men in the sketch, we can now reason that the working-class speaker continues to speak in the way he does partly because there is covert prestige in doing so. Just as the upper-class speaker uses his RP speech to help proudly locate him in his social group, so does the working-class speaker use his non-RP speech to help proudly locate *him* in *his* social group. Speech, along with other symbolic props such as the bowler hat or the flat cap, is being used as a way of presenting, performing, and inhabiting a particular identity.

But what about the middle-class character? He's interesting, because it tends to be middle-class people who try to adjust their speech 'upwards' in order to associate themselves with people of a higher social standing. William Labov, a sociolinguist who pioneered research into the relationship between language and social class, found that middle-class speakers even have a tendency to overdo what they perceive as 'correct' pronunciations (remember my grandfather and his 'shuggar'?).[3]

I realise this next example is extremely niche, and will only be recognised by a small group of probably British readers who watched a lot of TV in the early 1990s, but do you remember Hyacinth Bucket from the TV show *Keeping Up Appearances*? As a middle-class character from a lower-class background, desperate to climb the social ladder, she was the archetypal hypercorrecter. Everything she did, including her speech — a forced RP — was hypercorrect. One long-running joke was that she insisted that her surname was pronounced 'bouquet' rather than 'bucket'. She is a perfect, if over the top, example of someone using any resource available to her (speech, clothes, house décor) to appear to belong to a higher class. Sometimes she would use these resources appropriately, and sometimes she would be wide of the mark. Sometimes they would come across as painfully conscious and forced, and sometimes they would have become a natural, unconscious part of her everyday behaviour.

At the other end of the scale, you have people who adopt (consciously or otherwise) a markedly less prestigious or less standard way of speaking in order to gain a degree of covert prestige. They may also overdo it or misjudge the details, for example when, as already mentioned, well-to-do politicians slip into a 'mockney' (fake cockney) accent.

Of course, there is always the chance we are reading too much into all of this. Most of us, not counting Hyacinth Bucket, don't spend our time thinking about our social class and how we might want, or not want, to project that part of our identity at any given time. Some of us might only be dimly aware of the social class we are allegedly part of and feel that it doesn't really impact our behaviour, even if we understand its influence on shaping our lives. Others might be very conscious and possibly proud of the social class we identify with, but even that doesn't necessarily mean it is at the forefront of our minds as we go about our day-to-day business. One reason for this is that people tend to spend time with those similar to us. We behave, dress, and speak in similar ways to everybody else, more often than not in line with the norms of our particular social group. We aren't deliberately, or even consciously performing 'working class' or 'middle class' when we are hanging out with friends, we are simply hanging out. But when this is disrupted and people don't feel like they naturally fit in somewhere (such as a workplace or university) because of their accent, they may conclude that they are not welcome, and steer clear of those spaces.

Pink words and blue words

Whether we are cisgender, transgender, non-binary, or any of the many gender identities out there, our voice is one way in which we reflect this aspect of ourselves. For some, especially trans men and trans women (although not *only* or *all* trans men and trans women), it can be a crucial element of signalling gender identity; for others, it won't be at the forefront of our minds, but it will probably subconsciously play into how we speak nonetheless.

But to what extent do men and women actually speak differently? If you asked a child to imitate a man or a woman, they would probably attempt an especially low-pitched voice for the man, and an especially high-pitched voice for the woman. And this would be a fair enough place to start — men tend to have lower-pitched voices than women, largely due to the physiology of some of the apparatus that helps to create speech (testosterone enlarges and thickens the vocal folds, meaning they vibrate at a lower speed, creating a lower pitch). But this is not always the case — there are plenty of women with voices that are lower in pitch than a lot of men's, and there are plenty of men with voices that are higher in pitch than a lot of women's. However, the assumption that there is always an inherent and obvious difference between men's and women's voices is part of an interesting pattern that arises when we look at how we view men's and women's speech.

> Many modern Western societies are obsessed with sex and gender. Right from the moment of conception we place huge importance on whether 'It's a girl!' or 'It's a boy!'. A child's life is filled with gendered names, clothes, bedding, and toys, and, when they get a bit older, by gendered activities, sports, and general expectations. Now, if you happen to fit into this (binary) system — if you are completely happy being identified as a girl or a boy and to go along with the gender expectations that surround you — then you might not really notice

its effect. But if you don't fit, and you start to see and question gender roles, behaviours, and expectations, the system can become oppressive.

Underpinning all this is the way language is used. If you are a parent, grandparent, carer, or someone who regularly comes into contact with young people, think about whether you speak to them in the same way regardless of their gender. If you do, then great. But I think that would be quite unusual. I know I often don't. Similarly, think about whether you have different expectations of the language they use. Are there some things its more acceptable for a boy to say than a girl? Why? And what about your expectations of other adults? Do you notice it more when some people swear aggressively compared to when other people do it? Do you expect this person to be more likely to use soothing language when comforting someone than that person? Have you ever been surprised at how often this colleague speaks up in meetings or their habit of dominating whatever conversation they find themselves in, or does their behaviour seem natural to you?

In her book *The Myth of Mars and Venus*,[4] linguist Deborah Cameron outlines the most common myths around gender and language:

1. Language and communication matter more to women than men; women talk more than men.
2. Women are more verbally skilled than men.
3. Men's goals in using language tend to be instrumental — about getting things done — whereas women's

tend to be interpersonal or relational — about making connections to other people. Men talk more about things and facts, whereas women talk more about people, relationships, and feelings.
4. Men's way of using language is competitive, reflecting their general interest in acquiring and maintaining status; women's use of language is cooperative, reflecting their preference for equality and harmony. Because of this, men's style of communicating also tends to be more direct and less polite than women's.
5. These differences routinely lead to 'miscommunication' between the sexes, with each sex misinterpreting the other's intentions. This causes problems in contexts where men and women regularly interact, and especially in heterosexual relationships.

You will undoubtedly have heard some, if not all of these, stated as fact. However, Cameron proceeds to challenge or debunk each one.[5] She demonstrates that, when dealing with any broad-brush behavioural claims about any group of people, the facts are far more nuanced, far more complicated, far more context-dependent, and far less extreme. She makes the point that, much like other areas of social research, the study of language and gender has had a historical bias towards the behaviour of white, western, middle-class people. Far from being universal truths about language and gender, the statements above relate to observations and intuitions about one specific social group. The truth is that there are many more similarities than differences between the way men and women speak (I mean, think about it — how would we get anything done if there weren't?), and the differences *within* gender groups are just as important, or even more important, as those *between* the groups. Because it's within gender groups that we can see differences to do with social class, ethnicity, and all the other social factors we've been looking out for, being played out.[6]

The fact that these inaccurate generalisations around language and gender are so widely believed creates an interesting situation. If we do find ourselves foregrounding aspects of our gender identity in a particular context through our voices, how do we do it? We might well find ourselves displaying some of those stereotypical features, purely because we want other people to pick up on cues we know they will recognise. We could be doing this subconsciously, or we could be doing this consciously in an effort to sound especially masculine or feminine to suit a particular situation. For example, a new member of a men's rugby team might feel the need to assert their masculinity by speaking in a way that ultra-masculine men apparently do, according to the article on the pop-psychology website he was reading; and by doing so, he ends up reinforcing a potentially harmful — at the least, untrue — stereotype. Similarly, a new member of staff invited to a pampering spa day with 'the girls' might feel the need to play an extra feminine role in a bid to fit in with their expectations of what such a day involves. Little does either know that the rugby players are just as likely to be softly reassuring one another after a lost match and the women are just as likely to be swearing loudly at each other; in other words, going against the stereotypical norms.

So, what do men and women really sound like? The fact is, gender is so intertwined with other social factors and with the surrounding context, that it's impossible to make accurate generalisations about how people might perform their gender identities through language. As with all social factors in relation to speech, what it means to sound 'more feminine' will depend on the person speaking, the people listening, the underlying cultural context, and the precise situation the people find themselves in. It's not simply a case of doing more of this supposedly feminine feature, or doing less of that allegedly masculine feature, whoever and wherever you are.

> Don't worry men, I've found some tips online that will help make you sound even more manly!
>
> 1. Speak slowly. Speaking fast makes you seem insecure. Speaking slower makes you seem more in control and by extension more masculine.
> 2. Increase the time between your words. If you're naturally speaking very quickly, imagine. There's. A. Period. After. Every. Word. Don't breathe or make any other noises in between.
> 3. Strengthen your neck. Stronger muscles will improve your posture if done right, and less tension means a lower pitched voice. It also has the added bonus of giving you a bigger neck which makes you look stronger.
>
> Don't say this book hasn't given you anything. Stay. Manly. Out. There. Guys!

Sibilants and sexuality

The link between sexual orientation and language is one that *can* exist for *some* people but does not exist for many others. For now, our focus will be on gay men in countries such as the

UK and the US.[7] There is no doubt that some gay men speak in a way that identifies them as such (we'll look at what this entails shortly, but I'm sure you all have a friend, colleague, or famous person in mind). However, there are also plenty of gay men who do not speak in a way that suggests they might be gay, and there are also plenty of straight men who speak in a similar way to the (apparently) identifiably gay men. Linguist Deborah Cameron and anthropologist Don Kulik describe this succinctly: 'Not all gay men have the "the voice" and not everyone who has "the voice" is gay.'[8]

So, what is this 'gay voice'? It has variously been described as including some or all of the following features. First, a greater pitch range. This could mean more movement within the regular pitch range but might also mean making use of falsetto (high-pitched, outside the regular pitch range) and creaky voice (the opposite — a kind of low, almost growling quality). Second, the average pitch may be higher overall compared to men who don't have 'the voice'. Third, the pronunciation of the 'sibilant' sounds 's' and 'z' as in sorry and cars, which can be both lengthened and pronounced more emphatically. And last, lengthened vowel sounds: 'That's amaaazing!'.

The reason we know that people perceive there to be a gay voice, and that 'not all gay men have "the voice" and not everyone who has "the voice" is gay' is that people have tested it. The linguist Erez Levon, for example, did so by digitally manipulating two voices (one gay, one straight) to see if they would be perceived as more or less 'gay', with mixed results. One particularly interesting effect was the order in which somebody heard a series of voices — if a gay voice appeared after a few straight ones, it was perceived as being 'more gay'.[9]

So, what's happening? Why do some gay men speak in a way which sounds gay to other people, and some don't? Or why do some straight men speak in a way that sounds straight to other people, and some don't? As with all the other social factors we are looking at — social class, gender, race and ethnicity, regional background — it is a combination of what we have been exposed to and, therefore, naturally adopted into our own speech on the one hand, and the extent to which we bring this related part of ourselves to the surface through our language, consciously or subconsciously, on the other. Just as in some contexts and with some people a person might want to emphasise their Australianness, their masculinity, or their class by drawing on speech features that are associated with those categories, another might want to emphasise their 'gayness' — to signal their engagement with LGBTQ+ culture and their alignment with a specific subcultural identity — by drawing on speech features that are associated, often stereotypically, with being gay. This might be a conscious effort, or it might be completely natural; it might be just in some situations, or it might be all the time. In other words, some men will acquire gay-sounding features regardless of whether they are gay or not, simply because that's what they have been exposed to growing up. Meanwhile, men who are gay might either adopt, or not adopt, speech features that emphasise that part of who they are.

> There is a really interesting documentary you can watch on the topic of a 'gay voice' by David Thorpe called *Do I Sound Gay?*[10] (and a much shorter *New York Times* 'Op-Doc' *Who Sounds Gay?*),[11] which explores some of the themes mentioned here. Thorpe's documentary is especially insightful as it explores both the positives

and negatives of sounding gay. It provides examples of people who don't particularly like their 'gay-sounding' voice, yet have come to terms with it, which arguably questions the extent to which people have control over the way they sound. But people do have control; often, they are simply limited by boundaries imposed in the process of acquiring language. If we naturally acquire a way of speaking that is perceived as gay, then this might be our default way of speaking (to the extent that there is such a thing), but we can still consciously and unconsciously manoeuvre within this to emphasise or de-emphasise particular features depending on the context.

But so far everything has been about gay men — what about gay women? Is there a clear 'lesbian voice'? Well, not really. At least not in the same way that there is an identifiably, albeit inconsistently used, gay voice in men. There has been some research that has suggested a tendency for some lesbian women to pronounce some vowels in slightly different ways, or for some lesbian women to use a slightly lower pitch range, and the linguist Lucy Jones has explored how a group of lesbian friends use specific cultural references to existing lesbian-associated stereotypes to help maintain particular identities.[12] But there is no doubt that overall, the results are rather mixed.

Clearly, as with a lot of academic research, the focus has been on white North American or British cisgender men. Research into voice among other groups within the LGBTQ+ community would be valuable — because the more we ask such questions, the broader will become our understanding of its role.[13]

'She doesn't sound [insert race here]'

The last big social factor that contributes to how we speak is race and ethnicity. I was about to say that, like gender, the relationship between language and race/ethnicity is complex, but I have a feeling that goes without saying. Both race and ethnicity are social constructs.[14] This might go against what you feel you've learned elsewhere — which might be that race is based in biology and genetics, and that ethnicity is social, but there simply isn't the biological and genetic evidence to support historical claims of clearly defined racial categories of people. If you want a quick bit of evidence to demonstrate that race is something society has created rather than something science has discovered, just consider the different ways in which some groups of people have been described as part of the US census over the years. In an online article for *Vox* in 2014, Jenée Desmond-Harris describes how people of Mexican birth or ancestry were considered 'white' until the 1930 census, how the definition of 'Black' could vary between states, and how 'Germans, Greeks, Irish, Italians, and Spaniards have all — either legally or as matter of public opinion — been excluded from the "white" category at some point'.[15] In contrast, in 2018 the discussion concerned whether people from the Middle East and North Africa would soon finally be able to avoid having to tick either the 'white' box or the invisible 'other' when describing themselves.[16]

So, like all the other factors we have discussed, race and ethnicity are socially constructed, and this construction is carried out by individuals and groups of people in relation to their own identities, as well as by societies at large in relation to the identities of others. And when something is socially constructed, language likely plays a role in that construction. Given all of this, it goes without saying that people of different racial or ethnic backgrounds who speak in different ways don't do so because of some inherent biological predisposition. A child will acquire an accent or dialect that is associated with a particular racial or ethnic group by being around other people who speak in that way, the same as any other accent or dialect. And just as with any other way of speaking, individuals, or groups of people, are able to emphasise some features, ignore other features, and ultimately use the language in a way that foregrounds and performs (or the opposite) their racial or ethnic identity at any given time. And also, just like any other way of speaking, this might be done consciously or unconsciously, depending on the speaker and the context they find themselves in.

Different racial and ethnic groups might have different relationships with one another across time, and even between generations, especially in the context of migration. At one time it might be important for people to maintain some kind of in-group identity which separates them from other groups, at another time it might be important to lessen those differences. For example, the first generation of a family to come to the UK from Bangladesh, perhaps a couple in their 20s who arrive in the 1970s, might actively do what they can to not stand out in an attempt to assimilate to their new environment. They might then encourage their children, who are growing up in the often-hostile anti-immigrant context of 1980s Britain, to do the same, seeing this as the best way to succeed. In terms of language, this means only using English, and rejecting the language and culture of their parents' home country. However, this generation might then have children growing up in the 2000s, when, although there are still racial tensions, Britain is markedly more diverse. This diversity gives the young people the confidence to reconnect with their grandparents' culture and use it as a way of expressing pride in their own heritage. And this pride would come through in the clothes, the behaviour, and, of course, the everyday speech of these young people as they negotiate their own in-groups and out-groups.

It isn't always clear how a particular language feature comes to be part of a variety of speech associated with a specific racial or ethnic group. Sometimes it can be due to the influence of another language (often called a 'heritage' language, although the term implies the language is something of the past, whereas it is likely still vibrant in parts of the community), but often it is simply down to the way a variety of speech has naturally developed, as with any other accent or dialect (remember all that linguistic mystery from Chapter 1?). But it is possible to identify features that belong to the speech of different racial and ethnic groups of people. Perhaps the most-studied variety has been African American English (also known as African American Language and previously known as African American Vernacular English), which has been the focus of sociolinguistic research since the 1960s. Features such as not using the verb 'to be' ('am/is/are') in places where it is usually used in 'standard' English, (for example, 'she here' instead of 'she's here'), and what's known as the previously mentioned 'habitual be', where a habitual action might be described as 'they be arguing' (meaning they are always arguing, not necessarily that they are arguing right at this moment), are well known. In fact, they are so well known that they have been adopted by other groups of people, especially young people, who may have no connection with that particular racial group, yet who draw on the culture for their own purposes. We'll look at this in more detail in Chapter 5.

An example of a feature from a so-called heritage language that might be present in the English of some speakers is what's called retroflex 't' and 'd'. In English, the 't' and 'd' sounds are produced by the end of the tongue making contact with the hard bit just behind our top teeth (called the alveolar ridge), stopping the flow of air, and then moving away to release the air and make the sound. You can try this yourself by saying *ten* or *den* slowly, and noticing what your tongue is doing. However, in other languages such as Urdu and Gujurati, the sounds are made with the tongue in a slightly different position. Instead of putting your tongue against the alveolar ridge, this time curl the tip upwards and backwards and make it touch the roof of your mouth. Now say *ten* and *den*. This is the retroflex 't' and 'd'. You should be able to hear the difference, and you will probably recognise the sound as one that makes up some of the accents around you.

One important aspect of ethnicity in relation to language that is often overlooked is that of whiteness. Just as people who have an accent or dialect that happens to be close to the 'standard' of whatever society they are part of often believe they in fact have 'no accent', people who have a racial/ethnic background that matches that of the dominant norm in society are often seen as not having an ethnic identity. The result is that in places like the US, the UK, Australia, and much of Europe, 'whiteness' is not viewed as being a race or ethnicity in itself. Rather, it is seen as an absence of race and ethnicity. And language, or at least, the perception of language by the dominant group in society, plays an important role in this. For example, European colonisers would describe the language of Indigenous populations as simplistic to bolster the perception of those people as either subhuman, or less evolved than the colonisers.[17] Time and time again, the languages of non-dominant populations (in this instance as determined along racial lines) are seen as diverging from what is seen as 'normal' or 'standard', and as something that is in need of fixing.

Two people who have been doing a lot of work in this area are Jonathan Rosa and Nelson Flores. As part of their call for a 'raciolinguistic perspective' towards the study of language, they demonstrate how whiteness is at the core of so much education. They give the example of the 'Standard English learner' screening process used in US schools with the aim of identifying students in need of mainstream English language development. The student listens to a list of 'Standard English' sentences being read aloud, and then they are told to repeat them or write them down. These responses are then compared with pre-prepared lists of the same sentences written in a variety of 'non-standard' ways, which are intended to represent racialised varieties of English (in this case African American, Mexican American, and Hawaiian American). A sentence in African American English, for example, might include 'she happy' rather than 'she's happy'. The idea is that by comparing the sentences, school administrators are quickly able to see how far an individual's language deviates from the standard and therefore how much remedial language tuition is required in order to move them towards that standard. Because remember, standard varieties of language are objectively more sophisticated than other varieties of language, and they have achieved their prestigious position in society through the natural rise to the top of things that are demonstrably and naturally good ... Oh, wait.

Speaking intersectionally

Although I've presented these social factors one by one throughout this chapter (region, nationality, social class, gender, sexuality, and race and ethnicity) to show how each of them relates to language, they obviously don't work alone. What we are talking about here is intersectionality: the idea that social categories are linked and cannot effectively be considered separately.[18] Intersectionality is especially relevant when considering any kind of discrimination or privilege (which we will be doing in the next chapter), but it is a useful way to think about social factors in any context. This is at the heart of identity in that there are numerous aspects which combine, intersect, and even conflict, that together make us who we are.

For example, a young, bisexual, Black man born in Birmingham is likely to have experienced very different societal expectations from an elderly, straight, white woman raised in colonial Nairobi. The cumulative effect of these experiences — of each person's intersectional identity — will have had an effect on the way they speak.

And if we consider identity in this way, we might recognise that these two people might adjust the way they speak to foreground one or more of their many intersecting characteristics, depending on the situation.

Meanings upon meanings

But what about all the associations that exist between spoken language and other social groups, personalities, and behaviours, apart from the big demographic sets we've already covered? What about the speech features that are associated with being calm, or tough, or dismissive, or stand-offish? They might be slightly different for different groups of people, but they all exist. But how does this happen? Why do some speech features carry these associations, and others don't? And how do we know which ones to use?

If somebody asked you to imitate a 'well-spoken' person or character, what would you actually do? What would change in your voice? What about a 'tough' character, or a 'creepy' character, or a 'gangster' or a 'valley girl', or a 'jock', or a 'roadman'? You might not be able to do them all — indeed, you might not know what some of them are! But it is likely that you would know how to adjust your speech in a way that at least gives an idea of how you imagine a few of these categories of people speak, in the same way that you could try to imitate people of a different social class (I'm not saying the imitation would be good, I'm just saying you would probably know where to start). And if people understand your impersonation, clearly they share (or are aware of) the same connection between speech features and social characteristics. But how did these connections come about? How do accents come to acquire this kind of 'social meaning' when they are, after all, simply a series of sounds, which carry no meaning in themselves?

When I say that speech sounds have no meaning by themselves, I really do mean no meaning at all. The sound 't' doesn't mean anything, it is simply a small section of speech that contributes to a word such as *butter*. However, when the 't' sound is replaced by a glottal stop, then we can say it does have a kind of meaning. Not the same sort of meaning as the word butter itself has, but it does convey some kind of information to the listener. This information isn't about the object being described (*butter* is butter whether the 't' is pronounced as a 't' or as a glottal stop). Instead, it provides social information about the speaker, as long as the listener is tuned in to hear it. Precisely what it says about the speaker is up for debate, but in the case of a glottal stop for 't' it will likely have something to do with regional background and/or social class.

What has happened is that the 't'/glottal stop sound has acquired social meaning. Language is, as we know, full of meaning, but not always in the most obvious ways. 'The cat's on the chair' has a straightforward, surface-level meaning: a cat (who we know already, hence 'the' cat and not 'a' cat) is sitting, standing, or lying on a particular chair. That being said, while the straightforward meaning is clear, the information such a sentence is intending to convey might be different depending on the context: maybe the cat was lost ('I've found it!'), maybe the cat isn't supposed to be on the chair ('Move, cat!'), maybe someone's about to sit on the cat in the chair ('Don't squash the cat!'). All of these are possible reasons to say 'the cat's on the chair'. Then, of course, you have examples such as, 'Honestly, it's no problem at all', which can mean anything from something really being no problem, all the way to, 'If you ask me to do this for you one more time we will actually fall out.' These meanings exist above and beyond the straightforward everyday literal meaning of the sentence, and their understanding depends on the context in which the speech happens: who is saying it to who, where they are, their relationship, and so on. The same is true when thinking about the social meaning of particular pronunciations or other spoken language features — they can be understood as indicating or meaning something above and beyond their everyday role as part of a word or utterance.

The process by which this happens is usually thought of as a series of associations. A simple example from British English might be that the pronunciation of a clearly articulated 't' in words such as *hat* and *butler* is associated with RP-speaking people. Those people might be associated with being privately educated, and their private education might be associated with being posh. As a result, the clearly pronounced 't' becomes associated with poshness. What started as a small chain of associations has, therefore, become a single association between a particular pronunciation and a social characteristic. There is of course nothing inherently 'posh' about the sound of a clearly articulated 't' (which is, after all, simply created by placing the tip of the tongue against a particular part of the roof of the mouth and then releasing it), but it gains that social meaning through the process of associations. But these associations only work if we are all on the same page when it comes to our awareness of the society we are in. An outsider to Britain might make none of the associations described above when it comes to the 't' sound. To them, it will simply sound like 't'.

The point is, there are no fixed rules for how speech features are interpreted. Social meaning isn't fixed. Instead, it exists somewhere between, within, and among the speaker, the listener, and their combined understanding and experience. If someone is actively using a speech feature in order to help create a particular identity, it will only work if the people listening 'get' the reference. Similarly, different people will notice and interpret different speech features differently depending on their prior knowledge and familiarity. For example, someone from London might hear a Manchester accent and think 'working class and unsophisticated', while someone from the US might hear the same accent and think 'posh and refined'. One is picking up on the accent's northernness and attaching it to some stereotypical characteristics, from a southerner's perspective, and the other is picking up on the accent's Englishness and some stereotypical characteristics that can partner with that, from a US perspective.

One important aspect of the creation of any association between a speech feature and a social group, behaviour, or attitude is of course repetition. Imagine if, on meeting British aristocracy for the first time you hear someone pronounce a particular word in an especially unexpected way (maybe they say 'hellooooo' when they see you, maybe they make a clicking sound when they laugh, maybe they pronounce all their 's's like 'z's — I don't know what these people do!). You might think nothing of it other than, 'Hmm, that's a bit odd.' And if that was your one and only encounter with this person doing this thing, then that would be the end of it. He'd simply be 'that posh bloke who clicks'. But when you hear other people from the same background doing it again and again you start to see things differently. It becomes a thing that you associate with this particular group of people, and a thing that the people themselves see as a way of helping maintain a group identity.

If we go back to our discussion of broader social categories, we see the same thing happening. Speech features become associated with specific groups through those groups repeatedly using them. Not because there is anything intrinsically feminine/middle-class/gay about them, but because that's the association that develops when particular people use them again and again. And when this association has been made, these features can be used by others to help create that identity for themselves. Linguist Miriam Meyerhoff describes the process well in relation to masculinity. She says, 'A speaker uses one [speech feature] more than another, not because he *is* male, but because in speaking like that he is *constituting* himself as an exemplar of maleness, and constituting that [speech feature] as an emblem of masculinity.' Again, we create who we are, in part, through the way we speak.

We can take this further and argue that not only do we create who we are through language, but we also create the social world that surrounds us. The language we use to refer to and describe other people, ourselves, our relationships, our experiences, and our attitudes helps to make them real. In some cases, this reality only exists in the form of language. Our attitudes towards particular people, places, or behaviours may never be made concrete through action; they may simply exist as feelings, thoughts, and words. But their effect is no less real. However, because of the ways in which language can be endlessly interpreted, reinterpreted, and misinterpreted, those realities aren't always viewed or experienced in exactly the same way by each of us. When we start viewing language as having the power to not only create different versions of reality, but to actually create different realities, then we really do have to give it the attention it deserves. Because when we do this, we begin to understand how the ways we choose to use language perpetuate some deeply concerning inequalities.

CHAPTER 3

Prejudice and discrimination: how accents can hold us back

Has anybody ever criticised or mocked the way you speak? Maybe you have been the one doing the mocking. I mean, we all like and dislike all sorts of things, and that's fine, right? There's no crime in disliking this or that particular way of speaking. It's not like it's real prejudice against actual characteristics such as gender, ethnicity, or social class? Is it?

Now it's time to go a bit further into the darker side of accents. It's time to start exploring how people use the way other people speak as a way of judging, and even discriminating against, whole sections of society. Because they do. For example, a recent study found that 30 per cent of university students in the UK reported having been mocked, criticised, or singled out in educational settings due to their accents, rising to 40 per cent in social settings.[1] In another study it was found that people with 'foreign' accents were judged less credible than those with 'native' accents when re-telling statements of trivia,[2] and a piece of research from 2019 showed that in a mock-up of a legal trial, Black American defendants with a 'stereotypical' African American accent were more likely to be found guilty than defendants with other accents.[3]

But why should this be? Do some accents really make people sound less intelligent, more guilty, more attractive, and less trustworthy than others? Or is there perhaps a bit more to it?

Oh my God, I love a British accent!

You won't have to do much searching online to find news stories about regional or national accents with headlines like:

> 'NEW ZEALAND NAMED SEXIEST ACCENT IN THE WORLD!'[4]

> 'BIRMINGHAM ACCENT RANKED LEAST ATTRACTIVE IN THE UK – AND EVEN WOLVERHAMPTON IS HIGHER'[5]

> 'SCOUSERS HAVE THE "LEAST INTELLIGENT AND LEAST TRUSTWORTHY" ACCENT — WHILE DEVONIANS HAVE THE FRIENDLIEST'[6]

> 'BOSTON ACCENT RANKED MOST ANNOYING IN AMERICA'[7]

Every few months, a story will do the rounds reporting on a survey, often one commissioned by a travel or communications company, that asks people which accent they consider the most or least attractive/friendly/intelligent/trustworthy/sexy. In the UK, this is bad news for people from Liverpool or Birmingham, as their accents invariably come near the bottom. In the US, Texans might have an extra spring in their step, knowing that people find their accent 'sexy'. Although it is easy to dismiss such superficial research, when similar, more rigorous studies are carried out, we can see equally strong patterns emerge, although often with a bit more detail. For example, while a Received Pronunciation or BBC accent might come higher than a Newcastle accent on a measure of perceived intelligence, the two are likely to swap places on a measure of perceived friendliness.

But why are some accents consistently perceived as being more prestigious, friendly, or intelligent than others? As we have already seen, there are certainly no objective linguistic reasons. Rather, the various hierarchies of accents are built up over time through the repetition of existing attitudes and stereotypes, and passed on from one generation to the next. By this, I don't mean that there is some kind of ceremony where parents present their 18-year-old with the list of accent prejudices that have been in their family ever since they can remember and that are now the responsibility of the next generation to carry on. Rather, I mean that existing attitudes and stereotypes become part of general social awareness and understanding.

The findings of studies researching people's attitudes towards accents should be viewed with varying degrees of seriousness, depending on how they are carried out. Many of the less sophisticated approaches don't take into account the obvious biases that will exist depending on where the person assessing the accents is from. For example, some ingrained attitudes involve specific inter-regional grievances that may have nothing at all to do with voice, such as the rivalry and half-serious mistrust between places such as Liverpool and Manchester, Lancashire and Yorkshire, Sydney and Melbourne. However, even the most lighthearted and apparently flippant investigations can still serve a purpose, even if that purpose is simply to highlight that such stereotypes exist. For those of us who are interested in such things, people's stated views on accents are always relevant, however they are presented. Although having said that, when I recently saw a survey that asked, 'Which famous Chris's accent makes him most attractive?' followed by a bar chart labelled with the faces of actors Chris Evans, Chris Hemsworth, and Chris Pratt, I did have to quietly wonder what I was doing with my life.

There are two main ways to examine people's attitudes to accents. The first and most straightforward is to simply ask people to rank a list of accents from best to worst. You could also ask for those accents to be rated according to particular criteria, such as pleasantness or prestige, or perhaps for the speakers of those accents to be rated based on perceived attractiveness or intelligence. A simple version of this will be what is used to generate the headlines above, when a poll pops up on your social media asking, 'Which of these accents do you find the sexiest?' The results will be put out as a press release by the company that commissioned the 'research' and picked up by various news outlets to be shared widely and commented on by their readers. This suits everyone — news outlets get a quick story, people get to read and talk about accents while having their own prejudices confirmed, linguists like me get to go on the radio and discuss the results, and the travel or dating or communication company that commissioned the research gets their name out there for a couple of days. Everyone is happy. Oh, except the people in Birmingham and New Jersey, who are once again reminded of their apparent misfortune.

A more sophisticated and 'serious' version of this kind of research was carried out on a much larger scale in the UK in 2004 by linguists Nikolas Coupland and Hywel Bishop.[8] In collaboration with the BBC, they surveyed over 5,000 people on their views of 34 accents — their pleasantness (social attractiveness) and prestige. They found that the same four accents were ranked in the top five for both social attractiveness and prestige: 'Standard English', 'Accent identical to own', 'Scottish', and 'Edinburgh', with prestige then being joined by 'Queen's English' in top spot, and 'Southern Irish' joining the top list for social attractiveness. There were also similarities at the bottom of the lists, with the bottom three for social attractiveness being 'Birmingham', 'Black Country' and 'German accented English', and the bottom three for prestige being 'Birmingham', 'Asian'(!) and 'Black Country'.

There are clear and acknowledged drawbacks with this type of research, even when carried out properly. Most importantly — how can we be sure of what people are actually evaluating? After all, the people taking part aren't being asked to listen to people speaking, and evaluate what they hear, they are simply being asked to evaluate labels which broadly describe how someone speaks. But do we all interpret those labels in the same way? What I imagine when I think of a 'Birmingham' or a 'German' accent might be completely different from what you imagine. And what about a 'British' accent in a US survey, or the 'Asian' accent described in the study above? Which British or Asian accent are we talking about? Does everybody actually know what all the accents sound like? Maybe someone rated a particular accent negatively simply because they associate it with someone they don't like. But then again, can we ever separate the accent from the speaker? When we listen to someone speaking and we think or say that we like or dislike their accent, is it really the accent we are focusing on, or is it the speaker?

It's possible to infer from this type of research that if someone was told that the new person at work who is starting today has a 'Birmingham' accent, or a 'New York' accent, or even just an 'Australian' accent, they will form an opinion of this new person before they've even met them. Talk about prejudging — this person will be prematurely evaluated not even based on the way they speak, but on a description of the way someone says they speak.

One more thing to mention about the Coupland and Bishop study is that 'Accent identical to own' ranked near the top of both lists. This is a common finding in accent studies, and it makes intuitive sense. Whether it's borne out of a sense of regional pride, identity, or just familiarity, people tend to rate their own accent quite highly. Of course, this also ties in with the fact that people often think they 'don't have an accent', so it could be seen as a judgement on people who speak 'normally' ('like me') and people who don't ('like them'). Interestingly, in Coupland and Bishop's study, men chose 'Accent identical to own' more than women did.

An updated version of this study has recently been carried out by Accent Bias Britain, which surveyed over 800 people in relation to 38 accent labels.[9] Overall, they found a strikingly similar pattern to the 2004 study, with 'standard' accents appearing at the top, and Birmingham at the bottom. They then compared both sets of results to an even earlier study reported in 1970, and found equally consistent patterns, indicating that views haven't really changed in the UK over the last 50 years. However, Accent Bias Britain does offer one shred of positivity, which is that the differences between the overall top and bottom scores are slightly smaller in their study than in either of the previous studies, suggesting that while biases clearly still exist, they are perhaps not as strong as they once were. This is likely a result of increased exposure to different ways of speaking in our modern everyday lives.

The other main way of examining people's attitudes towards accents is by asking people to listen to them. Now, you might think this is simply a case of getting samples of voices with a range of accents, playing them to some willing participants, and asking them to rate the accents. The problem with this is that you can never be completely sure that people are evaluating the voices on regional accent alone. Maybe the person in the 'Liverpool' recording has a particularly pleasant-sounding voice that is less to do with its Liverpoolness and more to do with its tone. Or maybe the voice from Sydney is saying something your listener fundamentally disagrees with, so it becomes hard to separate the content from the accent. In both cases, it isn't necessarily the regional accent itself that is generating the positive or negative attitudes. The way researchers get around this is to use voices that are as similar to one another in every other aspect apart from regional accent. They might choose to use voices from women only, all of a similar age, all speaking on the same topic in a similar style, but all with different regional accents. That way, the researcher can be reasonably confident that any ratings are to do with the accent rather than the speaker (as far as this is possible).

A clever variation on this experiment is called a 'matched guise test'. Here, the listener is faced with a number of recordings of people with different accents saying the same thing, much like above. However, two of the voices are actually the same person using two different accents! The listener doesn't know this, and as long as these two voices are mixed up with the other voices, they usually don't notice. The thinking behind the approach is that any difference in rating between these two particular voices must surely be down to accent alone, as every other variable (such as voice quality, pitch, speed, and clarity) has been accounted for.[10]

Often, when people ask what I do for a living and I explain that I research, teach, and write about the way people speak, the person I'm talking to will first share their pet language peeves (for example, 'could of', 'pacifically', 'like', or 'dropping "t"s') and then tell me their favourite regional or national accent. They also tell me their least favourite accent, but they do usually start with their favourite, which I guess is a good thing. Depending on who it is and where we are, I will either nod along politely albeit with a face that says 'hmm, I don't quite agree with you but let's not ruin your kid's birthday party by going into why', or I will gently challenge them a little on why those language features bother them, and why they like or dislike those particular accents.

On the subject of language peeves, I'm not particularly sympathetic, and while I fully understand where they come from and why people feel they are important, it won't take much for me to dig a bit deeper and question their motives. But a favourite accent, is that really so bad? I mean, if somebody said that they love it when people pronounce *espresso* as 'expresso', then surely that's better than if they said they hated it. On the one hand, a favourite accent is no different to a favourite scent — you simply like the way it smells. You know some people don't like it, but that's fine, because you do. It just happens to be a personal preference of yours. On the other hand, a favourite accent is nothing like a favourite scent. A scent does not have the same social baggage attached to it; a scent is not a part of a person's identity (at least not in the same way). If you start prioritising your favourite scent over all the other scents, nothing bad will happen, you'll just end up with a lot of rose or lemongrass in your life. But if you start prioritising and favouring people with a particular accent over people with different accents, this will lead to inequality.

Now, I know what you're thinking: not all of us are in positions where we are regularly asked to 'choose' one person over another. We are not all employers who, when hiring staff, might be influenced by a person's accent. At most, we might decide that we are vaguely drawn to that salesperson rather than that salesperson because they seem friendly and trustworthy, and 'oh, because I do like an Irish accent'. In which case, why should it matter if you have a favourite accent? My response is that while it doesn't perhaps matter in individual situations, we should at least reflect on our preferences and consider the wider context. If there are accents we like more, then by definition, there must be accents that we like less. And if we are subtly treating people whose accents we like more favourably, we are probably treating those whose accents we don't like less favourably. And if we're not alone in doing this, the effect becomes cumulative and systemic. So, while we might tell ourselves that liking this or that accent is simply a harmless preference, the fact that it can affect how we treat people suggests that we really should think about where those preferences come from.

It's your voice, love. I don't like it.

It's not just accents associated with a particular region that people can take issue with. On 30 July 2021, during the Tokyo

Olympics, these tweets appeared, written by a man called Lord Digby Jones:

> Enough! I can't stand it anymore! Alex Scott spoils a good presentational job on the BBC Olympics Team with her very noticeable inability to pronounce her 'g's at the end of a word. Competitors are NOT taking part, Alex, in the fencin, rowin, boxin, kayakin, weightliftin & swimmin
>
> She's hot on the heels of Beth Rigby at Sky [and] the Home Secretary for God's sake! Can't someone give these people elocution lessons? I fear that it may be aped by youngsters along the lines of the use of the moronic interrogative originally caused by "Neighbours"; on behalf of the
>
> English Language.....Help!

Little did he know (actually, he probably did), what a stir this was about to cause over the following few days.

Let's unpack it a bit, as there is every reason you might not know all the characters and references in this little linguistic drama. First, Lord Digby Jones. Jones is a businessman, who, over the years, had various roles as an adviser to high-profile companies before entering the House of Lords in 2007 and briefly becoming a government minister. He retired from the House of Lords in 2020, aged 65. Alex Scott is an ex-footballer who played for Arsenal and the England national team, retiring in 2017, aged 33. She then began a career in TV, covering football and other sports, and by 2021 she was one of the main presenters on the BBC's coverage of the Olympic Games. As for the two minor characters — Beth Rigby is political editor for Sky News, and Priti Patel was the Home Secretary at the time of Digby's tweet.

As for the content of the tweets, Jones is clearly troubled about Scott dropping her 'g's — a common (although technically inaccurate) description of when somebody pronounces words ending in 'ing' as if the 'g' was missing from the spelling. Rigby and Patel get drawn in because they are two more women (yes, this point is relevant) who also display this language feature. The reference to 'Neighbours' and the 'moronic interrogative' is a bit of a wildcard. It refers to the misguided belief mentioned in Chapter 1 that watching too much of this Australian TV soap caused young people in the 80s and 90s to start using rising intonation at the end of sentences, as if they were asking a question. Its inclusion is interesting though, as it suggests that Jones is a man who routinely gets annoyed about certain language features, and that his anger at 'g'-dropping is not just a one-off.

Describing this language feature as 'g'-dropping or not pronouncing your 'g's is inaccurate as most people don't really pronounce the 'g' in words like *boxing*, certainly not in the way we pronounce the 'g' in *bag*. Sure, if the 'g' was not there in the spelling, the word would look like 'boxin', and we would probably pronounce it as such, but by adding the 'g', we are not adding another sound to the pronunciation. We don't pronounce the 'n' and then the 'g'. Instead, the 'g' indicates that the nature of the final sound of the word is different, and it is neither an 'n' or a 'g', but somewhere in between. This is where we need to use some fancy symbols. As we know, English has about 44 sounds, but only 26 letters, which makes our written language quite inefficient at representing the sounds of speech. In order to represent these sounds, we use a set of symbols. Some of the symbols are the same as the letters we already use, but when writing them we always put them in slashes. The sound /d/ for example is the one we associate with the letter 'd' in *dog*, and the sound /s/ represents the 's' in *sit*. But then there are less familiar symbols such as /ʃ/ which represents the 'sh' sound in *sheep*, or /ŋ/ which represents the 'ng' sound in words like *boxing*. The sound is between an 'n' and a 'g', and so the symbol is a mixture of the two. If you still aren't sure of what I mean, make a /n/ sound (as in *now*) and think about what your tongue is doing in order to produce it. You should find that the tip of your tongue touches the bit just behind your top teeth, where you can hold it and make the /n/ sound as long as you like. Now make a /g/ sound (as in *go*) and think about what's going on. You should feel something closing and then releasing in the back of your mouth near your throat. Now make the /ŋ/ sound as in *sing*. You should feel a different kind of contact, again towards the back of your mouth, that you can hold for a long time, like the /n/.

There is one more fascinating detail to add to all this. Even though I just said we don't really pronounce the 'g' in words like *boxing*, some people actually do. I explained earlier in the book that some accents in England, especially in the north-west and the midlands, the 'g' is indeed sounded, but after the /ŋ/, so its actually written /ŋg/. This is one of those accent features that most people don't notice, so it is only when somebody points it out that a non-'g'-user will say 'really, you pronounce the 'g'?' and a 'g'-user will shrug and say 'how can you not?'. For people who use this pronunciation, the words *anger* and *hanger* will rhyme. This means that there are actually three ways of pronouncing 'ng' words: /ŋ/ as in 'boxing', /n/ as in 'boxin' and /ŋg/ as in 'boxinG'. This last one makes the idea of 'g'-dropping even more nonsensical, as in one sense, everybody who doesn't have that additional feature is actually dropping their 'g's all the time.

The fact that people refer to this accent feature as 'g'-dropping is really due to the dominance of written language over spoken. For many people, writing is somehow seen as the 'real' and 'proper' version of English, and speech is seen as secondary. But this makes no sense. Writing was originally simply a way of recording spoken language (remember all that variation in spelling I mentioned in Chapter 1). When people hear 'boxin', they think of the spelling and decide that the speaker is simply missing out the 'g', often putting this omission down to laziness, poor education, coming from a lower social class, or a combination of all three. But what is actually happening is far more interesting, and not at all lazy. In fact, there was a time when this pronunciation was associated with the upper rather than lower social classes, at least in England. The phrase 'huntin', shootin', and fishin'' is often used to refer to a group of upper-class men who used a particularly conservative type of RP in the early 1900s (and who also enjoyed those kinds of activities). The style is famously captured in the speech of Dorothy L. Sayers' fictional amateur detective Lord Peter Wimsey. Funnily enough, so-called 'g'-dropping wasn't seen as lazy when they did it. Maybe it's not about the sound itself after all. Maybe it's more about who is using the speech feature and how we perceive them, than it is about the actual speech feature. If the speaker is 'one of us', the feature's status is reinforced as normal and correct, but if the speaker is not 'one of us', the feature's status is relegated to being lazy and incorrect. And a great example of the fluidity and arbitrariness of the relationship between a particular speech sound and what it can represent is 'g'-dropping's journey across the English class system in the last 100 years.

Jones' tweet caused quite a reaction. On the one hand, there were lots of people agreeing with him. Many of them took the opportunity to mention all the other features of English that they think are used incorrectly, or all the other people who, in their opinion, speak English badly. People with such viewpoints will often declare themselves as unashamed language pedants (although some will mistype this as pendants, which is always funny), protecting our language from misuse and deterioration. Some of them also took the opportunity to criticise Scott further for other aspects of her language and presenting style. On the other hand, the Twitter linguists, language specialists, and enthusiasts (combined, we are a small, usually polite, but often vocal group) wasted no time in pointing out why this was a particularly bad take. Our main role in this context is to remind people that linguistic variation is natural, that there are lots of different accents and dialects, that notions of 'correctness' when it comes to speech are borne out of historical privilege rather than linguistic superiority, that our accent is a big part of who we are and to bear that in mind when you criticise the way someone speaks. In the case of Jones and Scott, we also highlighted the imbalance of power at play. Jones is an older, privately educated, white, male peer complaining about the speech of a younger, state-school educated, Black, female sports presenter. In 2021, Scott may have more cultural relevance and social capital than Jones, but society continues to position the levers of real power in the hands of people like him rather than people like her, so Jones criticising Scott's speech is viewed as 'punching down'. Jones was seen as allowing his negative views on young, Black, working-class women in prominent positions to come through via his criticism of her speech.

> Now, some of you might feel this is a bit strong, and that this is an overly critical reading of someone simply commenting on a TV presenter's speech. I disagree, but I can see how taking this kind of approach in other situations might be problematic. I think we should argue as fiercely as we like when we are discussing language that is discriminatory, but admit that 'language people' can sometimes display an unhelpful single-mindedness in rooting out more everyday examples of linguistic criticism. I worry sometimes that we are so immediately critical of those who comment on the speech of others, that we risk not properly getting our reasoning across. After all, for a lot of us it has taken time (and reading and reflection and someone explaining it to us) to see how preferences about different speech features actually go a lot deeper than speech itself. So we shouldn't assume that other people will immediately make that connection simply because we jump in and say it's there. My point is, if we go charging in every time saying that this or that comment is discriminatory without properly explaining why, then at best people won't engage, and at worst we will be further entrenching the different viewpoints. Admittedly, given that the usual contexts for these discussions do not lend themselves to nuanced debate (social media, a quick radio or TV interview, or a quote in a newspaper story), it can be hard to put forward a

> sophisticated argument. But I do sometimes think we need to be better than simply saying 'You're wrong. This is classist/sexist/racist/homophobic/transphobic' without being able to a) demonstrate how, and b) acknowledge that people often have very deep-seated views on language that might take a bit of thought to challenge effectively.

The third group of people who got involved in the Jones/Scott debate questioned why Scott's pronunciation of 'ing' was relevant to anyone, and why this man was getting so irate about it. These are good people. These are people who allow us to believe that there is light at the end of the tunnel of language-based prejudice. For some, their viewpoints might be informed by linguistic awareness, but in many ways, I hope this isn't the case. It's reassuring to think that even without a detailed understanding of the history of accents and the vagaries of prestige, there are people who simply question why one person would criticise another on the basis of something so utterly arbitrary as the way they pronounce certain words.

Actually, just think about that last point. When we criticise the way someone pronounces particular words, just consider for a moment precisely what is happening. We are making judgements about a person and ascribing them all sorts of characteristics, often negative, purely because they pronounce particular sounds with their tongue or lips in a slightly (and we're talking millimetres or fractions of millimetres) different position compared to someone else. It's pretty nonsensical when you put it like that.

Most of us probably aren't consciously thinking about where we're from or our social class in relation to how we are speaking all the time — we simply get on with it. However, when it does become conscious is when we are put in a situation where our social background becomes relevant for some reason, perhaps because it makes us stand out from people around us. I imagine we've all been in a situation where we feel out of place due to the surroundings and other people being 'posh' (okay, all of us except for posh people). This might be in a situation as relatively superficial as being invited to a prestigious event where everybody is dressed in a particular way and seems to know which cutlery to use and which wine glass is which. Or it might be something a lot more serious like feeling out of place in a new job or at a new university. Even if you are desperate to fit in and have worn the 'right' clothes and talk about the 'right' things and laugh at the 'right' jokes, as soon as you open your mouth you will be providing information that you might, for whatever reason, be trying to hide or play down. The fact is, if you have a strong 'regional' accent or an identifiably 'working-class' accent, you will be perceived as something out of the ordinary, as coming from a different, and possibly 'wrong', background.

Bizarrely, those perceptions of social class might actually be utterly misguided. So entrenched is the idea of RP being prestigious, that for some people any accent that is markedly different from that (and by this I mean any accent that isn't from south-east England, in a UK context) can be seen as working class. This is especially the case for accents from the north of England. The same is true the other way around, with some people from the north of England often seeing any accent that is even vaguely southern as 'posh'. There is a well-established north-south divide in England, with differences (albeit often contested) along social, cultural, and economic lines. Of the two broad areas, it is the south that is seen as prosperous. According to a report published in January 2022, London received investment equivalent to £12,418 per person in the five years up to 2019/20, while the north of England received £8,125 per person over the same period.[11] Some northern English accents automatically conjure up images of a harsh industrial and post-industrial environment (and others a bucolic lack of sophistication) along with all the stereotypes that go with it. While some southern accents bring to mind government, royalty, and all the stereotypes that go with the easy life of the home counties. Of course we know that the situation is far more complex than this, but the broad stereotypes remain. The result of this divide is that 'northerners' (northern England) will very likely be viewed as lower down the social scale by people in the south of England, and 'southerners' (southern England) will most likely be viewed as higher up the social scale by people in the north of England. I am obviously making a huge generalisation here, but it's one based on truth.

Speaking of huge generalisations, this is probably a good time to take a step back and question the way in which I've presented the idea of social class so far. If you read much of the research on social class and language, you will see people neatly divided into different groups such as working class, lower middle class, middle class and so on, in order to then explore language differences between them. This is fine to an extent, as long as we are dealing with people who are similar in other important respects such as gender, ethnicity, and nationality. Most research will indeed ensure this, and will additionally separate people according to those other criteria. This means that a lot of the findings, certainly the parts that are reported more widely, are based on one particular group of people within a class system. And in the UK and the US this has often, by default, been cisgender men or women who are clearly 'white British' or 'white American'.

What then happens is that we take the class divisions that were used for one group of people and apply them to other groups of people, trying to fit everyone into the same categories of social class. But this isn't how things work. Within a group of people who are identified as working class on the basis of income, housing, and employment for example, there will be different experiences of what this actually means in terms of everyday life, attitudes, and behaviour. A white British woman from Birmingham, a Black British man from Leeds, a young Polish woman from London who came to the UK when it was part of the EU, and a gay Iraqi man from Brighton who came to the UK seeking asylum, will potentially all have very different experiences of their British 'working class' category. It therefore starts to make less and less sense to make generalisations about, for example, 'working-class speech'. This doesn't mean we shouldn't explore it, far from it, it simply means that we should reflect on what it is we actually mean when we discuss it.

And so we're back to intersectionality, the inseparable nature of social categories. In the context of language, a working-class Black woman may face challenges due to the way she speaks, but these will not be the same as the challenges faced by a working-class white woman, or by a working-class Black man. In each situation, class, gender, race, ethnicity, sexuality, religion, (dis)ability, physical appearance, and so on intersect to create a specific context for each person.

One particularly interesting way in which the experience of social class, and language may differ according to other social factors is in the context of immigration. Put very simply — what happens when an individual who is identified as being part of one social class in one context, moves to another context in which they are identified as being part of a completely different social class? Do they retain their original social class, or is it all relative to where they are within this new context? And how does this affect someone's language? The situation is actually very common for some people coming to countries such as the UK, USA, or Australia, who arrive either as economic migrants seeking a higher standard of living or as refugees. In both cases, there will be people who were part of a middle or upper-middle class in their home countries, but who now find themselves in less affluent working-class communities. Back in 2007, I carried out research looking at the extent to which Polish migrants to Manchester, UK, acquired a Manchester accent. Over the course of the research, I came across several people who had left demonstrably middle-class careers and lives in Poland because they learned they could earn more in the UK for less prestigious work, meeting their families' needs. Some were here to stay, some were here temporarily. The clearest example of a change in class-associated job was a Warsaw newspaper editor who had become a Manchester warehouse security guard. The reason this is interesting linguistically is because this person would probably speak in a middle-class version of Polish due to his career, education, and likely social context (I am reliably informed that although there is not as much class-based linguistic variation in Polish as in British English, there is some). Yet in England, he would probably acquire a variety of English that is associated with working-class speakers due to his new job, colleagues, and likely social context. This means that on language alone, a Polish person would hear him speak Polish and identify him as belonging to one social class, but an English person would hear him speak English and identify him as belonging to a different social class.

Incidentally, I should tell you an amusing story about that research. It was for my PhD, and I remember trying to explain what I was doing to my daughter, Maya, who was seven at the time. As I've mentioned elsewhere, Maya and I have noticeably different accents, as she grew up in Bolton, in the north-west of England, and I am from Hertfordshire in the south. I tried to explain the research by asking her to imagine someone who came to England from another country and started to learn English — would she speak like you, or like me? She thought for a bit and said, 'It depends on who her friends are. If she made friends with people like me, she would speak like me, but if she made friends with people like you, she would speak like you'. Which is absolutely right, only I was about to spend the next three years working out what the seven-year-old had (rightly) predicted in two minutes. I like to think I added an extra layer of sophistication and depth to the observation, but that's debatable. I did create some nice graphs though; take that, seven-year-old Maya!

The question of immigration complicates the relationship between social class and speech, but then so does another very common aspect of UK life — the fact that social class is not fixed. What about people who move from one identifiable class to another in the course of their lives? Perhaps the most common example of this is when people have a typically working-class childhood, only to later find themselves in a clearly identifiable middle-class adulthood. Here I'm thinking of individuals who were maybe the first of their family to go to university, and have now become doctors, teachers, or solicitors, or have gone into other professions most associated with the middle class. How do they identify in terms of social class? And what role does language play in this decision?

For many, the way they speak will be something they think about a lot. A newly qualified teacher from a working-class area of Leeds might feel acutely aware of the way they speak when they start a new post at a prestigious school in Surrey, for example. Whether or not that teacher then changes the way they speak, either consciously or unconsciously, depends almost entirely on personality and issues of identity. Personality, because it is likely that they will stand out for being different from many of the other teachers (who we can presume come from the local area). Some people don't mind being different, while some would much rather blend in with everyone else. Neither option is good or bad, it just means that the person who prefers to blend in will very likely find their accent (at least their work accent) adjusting to be less Leeds and more Surrey, perhaps ending up somewhere around general northern English in the process. It also depends on identity because the way we speak can be a way of performing and demonstrating pride in where we come from. It might even be the case that this teacher exaggerates their Leeds accent when in Surrey as a way of demonstrating their Leeds identity, and signalling that they are not about to change their accent for anyone. Which actually suggests a combination of personality and identity.

When it comes to teachers and accents, I know what some of you might be thinking: 'But what about when someone's accent is too difficult to understand? Should that be used in the classroom without any adjustments?' I don't think it's controversial to suggest that any teacher would see 'being understood' as a minimum requirement for a class to take place. However, I would like to suggest that being understood is not entirely, or even mostly, the responsibility of the speaker. It's only natural that if someone speaks in a way which we aren't familiar with, it might take a bit more effort to process what they are saying but once we make that effort and become more familiar, the issues will disappear.[12] After all, this person's friends and family understand them absolutely fine, and they probably use a much more pronounced version of their accent with them. So it really shouldn't take much for anyone else to get to the same point, especially when we remember that it is only relatively few sounds that differ between accents.

This is fundamental to understanding accent variation and prejudice. Too often when we think people should improve their speaking skills, we are focusing on the wrong thing. What we should really be focusing on is improving people's listening skills. Remember that a teacher from a working-class background in Hertfordshire, in the south of England, will probably never face this issue in relation to their accent, yet a teacher from a working-class background in Harrogate, in the north, might. Similarly, a Black or Asian teacher whose speech reflects their race and ethnicity in some way or whose speech is influenced by a language other than English, is much more likely to have their speech commented on than their white colleagues. That's surely a listener issue rather than a speaker issue. If we want to make society fairer in relation to spoken English, then we all need to get a lot better at listening. But in order to do that, we need to see and hear a wider range of people and voices across different professions and start challenging the preconceptions that exist around certain roles when it comes to the way people speak, especially when this relates to social class.

Thankfully, some professions, such as broadcasting and teaching, seem to be representing greater linguistic diversity than they did in the past. There is still some way to go — there are very few mainstream newsreaders on the BBC who do not have a modern RP or south-east England accent, and there are still stories about trainee teachers being told to change the way they speak and become less markedly 'regional' — but things seem to be moving in the right direction. However, other professions are a little more stuck in their traditional ways; for example, the legal profession.[13] Traditionally, barristers in England have tended to speak in Standard English dialects and RP (or similar) accents. This is an expectation of the role, and one that trainee barristers are encouraged to work to match, whatever their background. When it comes to dialect, this is understandable to an extent — the language of the court needs to be widely understandable, precise, persuasive, and, arguably, with a degree of formality that matches the seriousness of the context. At the moment, the dialect that matches that description is Standard English. However, the expectation that this language must be delivered using RP is less easy to accept.

Eloquence and persuasiveness are not restricted by accent. It is possible to speak eloquently and persuasively in any accent, which is, as we know, simply a system of sounds with which to pronounce the language. It is true that eloquence and persuasiveness are, to a certain extent, restricted by dialect; but only in terms of what is expected and understood within the context. It would be nonsensical to suggest that an elderly Yorkshire farmer could not use traditional local dialect to speak eloquently and persuasively, but this would not be understood as such in the context of the court. (Equally, it has to be said that an RP-speaking barrister addressing a group of elderly Yorkshire farmers would probably also be viewed with suspicion and miscomprehension.)

The insistence on, or tradition of, barristers speaking RP or similar makes an already exclusive and elite profession even more inaccessible to those with accents from other UK regions or with accents influenced by other languages that might be spoken at home or with family. It would be beneficial for people to hear their own voices represented in that context, whether they are future barristers or people caught up in the legal system. It would certainly help challenge some of the inherent class divisions that are maintained in part through language.

I once got into a discussion over this point with the barrister, broadcaster and author, Hashi Mohamed. In his writing and public speaking, Hashi makes the point that while we might like there to be greater diversity, and acceptance of diversity, at the Bar, it is better to deal with the world as it is, rather than as it should be.[14] In other words, while an individual with a markedly non-RP accent who wants to become a barrister might resent feeling pressured into adapting the way they speak in order to get ahead, they should not feel obliged to sabotage their careers for the greater good. It should not fall on their shoulders to attempt to change such an embedded system.

On the one hand, I completely agree — it is desperately unfair that some people are automatically at a disadvantage compared to others simply because of where they grew up. And then to be expected to shoulder the burden of challenging this inequality is clearly too much. But something does need to change. My feeling is that it should fall to those already on the inside, in the positions of power, to challenge the status quo. If every barrister who adapted their own way of speaking in order to get to where they are now started to revert back to their original way of speaking, then gradually the courtrooms would be filled not only with the sounds of RP, but with the sounds of Liverpool, Manchester, Glasgow, Nigeria, Somalia, and Bangladesh. And in time, the message would get out that yes, there are linguistic expectations of eloquence and persuasiveness at the Bar, but look at the wonderful phonetic and stylistic diversity with which this eloquence can be expressed![15]

Double standards? Now there's a surprise.

Alex Scott is not the only public figure who is criticised for the way they speak. As we've seen, Jones was quick to bring in Priti Patel and Beth Rigby as examples of others who could apparently do with elocution lessons. Then there's UK Member of Parliament and Deputy Leader of the Labour Party Angela Rayner, who routinely has to deal with comments and abuse online following any public appearance, much of it about her voice rather than what she is saying. Some people object to her working-class Stockport (north-west England) accent: when she speaks, the word *class* rhymes with *maths* and there is a glottal stop in *university*. Her critics are driven to distraction by the fact that she might say 'I was sat' rather than 'I was sitting', and newspaper articles have been written about the fact that she said, 'Was you there?' in a Radio 4 interview. Alexandria Ocasio-Cortez and Steph McGovern are other examples, as is Julia Gillard, ex-Australian Prime Minister, whose accent is, well, just too Australian for some.

Astute readers will have noticed a pattern in the examples I've presented here. They are all women, three are women of colour, and at least six are in jobs traditionally dominated by men (footballer turned pundit, government minister, political editor, member of parliament, US senator, prime minister). Admittedly, this is a hand-picked sample selected to illustrate a point, but there is no doubt that it is far easier to find examples of women facing comments of this sort than it is to find men. What's more, there are men in identical roles and with similar speech features who don't routinely get picked up on the way they speak (compare Alex Scott with Rio Ferdinand for example). It's almost as if there's a double standard in play (hard to believe, I know). Author and broadcaster Katie Edwards, who has faced her own share of unsolicited comments on her Doncaster accent from BBC Radio 4 listeners, suggests that for some men who have managed to get where they are 'despite' how they speak, 'a regional accent can become a strength and worn as a badge of honour, an emblem of their personal prowess ... For women working in the same sectors, however, having a regional accent can be far more difficult to negotiate ... Perhaps it's because speaking with a "rough" accent is unexpected; it's a transgression of ideal femininity. It's not "ladylike" and, no matter how much we regionally-vowelled women may rail against it, that becomes important because speech is a social symbol and we are judged on our pronunciation.'[16] Another reason for the disparity between the extent to which women and men are criticised for the way they speak is because women in the public eye are judged more frequently and more harshly for a whole range of things, from clothes, to appearance, to perceived ability. The linguist Deborah Cameron links this increased criticism to the fact that women are judged, to a far greater extent than men, by their perceived physical/sexual attractiveness.[17] Speech is part of this, hence a common criticism of women's voices being too 'shrill' or 'whiney', two especially unalluring adjectives. And it's not only women in the public eye who experience this. Speech is just one more piece of ammunition to be used in the ongoing battle to remind women that they don't belong in the positions of power they find themselves in.

Research shows that we tend to prefer leaders with lower-pitched voices, as we relate this speech feature to authority.[18] While this was shown to be the case for both men and women, it is arguably a more problematic finding for women, who tend to have higher-pitched voices. A famous example of a woman in power consciously deepening her voice was UK Prime Minister, Margaret Thatcher. There is some debate as to whether she worked with a voice coach or simply figured things out for herself, but whatever the process, it was a conscious decision.[19] And lowering the pitch of your voice to be taken more seriously as a woman in the workplace (along with adopting other more male-associated linguistic behaviours) is still a piece of advice that is regularly trotted out in online articles.[20] In 2016, the linguist Nic Subtirelu explored descriptions of then Presidential candidate Hillary Clinton's speech in the United States, which included adjectives such as 'shrill', 'screeching', and 'shrieking'. Arguing that these are gendered criticisms (compared to the 'passionate' or 'hard-hitting' speech of her male rivals), he explored the frequency at which these terms are used in US media. He found that women are 2.17 times more likely to be described as 'screeching' than men, 3.14 times more likely to be described as 'shrieking', and 2.3 times more likely to be described as 'shrill'.[21]

Vocal fry and uptalk are good examples of how additional social meaning can be attached to ways of speaking. Vocal fry, often called creaky voice, describes a way of speaking in which the pitch of the voice drops to an unusually low level, creating a growling, creaking effect where we can almost hear the individual vibrations that create the sound. It's one of those things that is far easier to demonstrate than describe so, as I said earlier, I encourage you to search online for 'Kim Kardashian creaky voice' and play some of the examples. You could also try Zooey Deschanel or Britney Spears, or the TikTok content creator @kateao4. The reason you search for Kim Kardashian is because she is routinely identified as the archetypal vocal fryer, so you will very quickly come across compilation videos of extracts of her speech that demonstrate this. However, do bear in mind that if you made a video of multiple decontextualised examples of any speech feature from absolutely any speaker, it would sound utterly ridiculous. Imagine if someone made a compilation video of all the times you say 'hmm', it would sound equally odd. It is true that Kim Kardashian uses vocal fry a lot, but then so do a lot of other people. And even more people use it a bit, even you.[22]

If, after you've watched a Kim Kardashian video, you continue to do some online research around vocal fry, you will find article upon article, blog post upon blog post explaining how it is a feature of young women's speech (especially American women), that it is incredibly annoying, and that it damages their job prospects as people won't take them seriously. Let's take these points in turn.

How to do vocal fry
Open your mouth and relax. Make a long 'uh' sound, but with as little energy as possible. Imagine you're an extra in a cheap zombie movie, or you've just woken up from a bad night's sleep. Aim for a low-pitched

growling sound and remove any kind of tone from your voice, until you can almost hear and feel the individual pulses of your vocal folds vibrating. That sound is vocal fry. Now that you can hear it and feel it, you can try to use it without having to look like a zombie. It is very likely that you'll realise you do in fact use it anyway, likely at the ends of phrases, or when your speech slows down.

Yes, young women use vocal fry, and some of them use it a lot. But so do men. And we're not just talking about men who have similar lifestyles and have the same social influences as Kim Kardashian. In fact, some men who use it have spectacularly little in common with Kim Kardashian at all. When I teach my students about vocal fry, I do indeed use a clip of Kim Kardashian to illustrate what it is. But this is quickly followed by another clip of a lesser-known vocal fryer — Jacob Rees-Mogg, British politician and member of parliament for North East Somerset. If you don't know who Jacob Rees-Mogg is, he's traditional (or old-fashioned) in every sense of the word — in his political views, in the way he dresses, and in the way he speaks, which is a remarkably posh RP. I think it's safe to say that Kim and Jacob are at opposite ends of a spectrum. I'm not sure what spectrum precisely, but I don't imagine their paths will ever cross, or that Kim would have the slightest clue who Jacob is. In between Kim and Jacob there are plenty of other well-known men who provide good examples of vocal fry: Benedict Cumberbatch, Bradley Cooper, Jeff Bridges, your dad (probably), to name a few.

So why is vocal fry still associated with young women? The

most likely reason is the tendency for young women to be the ones responsible for popularising 'new' language features. This has been shown time and time again in sociolinguistic studies — where there is a community of people in which a new pronunciation, word, or grammatical structure is emerging, then it is very often younger women who are using the feature first.[23] Precisely why (and to what extent) young women in particular have adopted vocal fry is up for debate, and there are plenty of linguists working to better understand it.[24] But it is undoubtedly being used to signal some kind of social alignment to a particular group, or to indicate a particular attitude in a given context. Its precise social meaning will depend on the environment in which the young women operate, but there is no doubt that it is contributing to the enactment of identity in one way or another. Which, once again, should make you start to question the motivation and the effect of such intense criticism. Are we criticising the language or the speaker?

Language change and innovation is never neat and tidy, but the general pattern of young women to older men is the one that is most often observed. The reason it is important to know that Jacob Rees-Mogg in particular, but also other men, use vocal fry in their speech is because this fact challenges the general discourse around how the speech feature is widely perceived. If we are continually told it is only young women who do it, then that is all we notice; we interpret what we see in relation to our expectations. It is a version of the 'frequency illusion', where the combination of selective attention (we notice things that are important to us, or that we are interested in) and confirmation bias (the tendency to interpret new information as confirming our existing beliefs and disregard information that challenges them) means that once we learn about vocal fry and that it is something young women do, that's all we see. It means we notice this woman doing it on-screen rather than this man, we notice our daughter doing it rather than our son, when in fact we might all be doing it.

To be fair, we can justify the fact that people tend to notice vocal fry in women more than they do in men to a certain extent on the basis that men's speech tends to be at a lower pitch than women's speech. Given that vocal fry is created by the voice dropping to a low pitch, the shift to vocal fry for men is often less noticeable than it is for women, whose voices tend to be higher.

However, this doesn't at all account for the second issue — that people find vocal fry annoying. Surely if a speech feature itself is objectively annoying, then it must be annoying whoever is doing it. But younger women clearly don't find each other annoying when they do it; quite the opposite, as they are probably using it as a way of indicating group solidarity. And the fact that the shift in pitch when using creaky voice is greater for a lot of women than it is for a lot of men is irrelevant; if people find Kim Kardashian annoying on the basis of her creaky voice, then it follows that they should find Benedict Cumberbatch annoying on the basis of his creaky voice. But they don't. And Jacob Rees-Mogg might be criticised for lots of things, and I have no doubt many people find him annoying, but I'm not aware of anyone singling out his creaky voice as the reason for it. In women, vocal fry is an irritating affectation. In men it is, we're told, just the way they speak.

The third issue is related to the second — that vocal fry is damaging women's job prospects as people won't take them seriously. This is one of those views that is constantly regurgitated in the media, and sometimes even in schools. The reason it gets so much traction is that it appeals to many people's common sense — 'I notice this speech feature a lot in young women (that is, now that you've pointed it out to me; I must admit I wasn't really aware of it before you explained it and showed me that video of Kim Kardashian)'; 'I find it annoying (because, erm, I just do)'; 'if I were employing someone I would definitely choose someone who doesn't sound like this over someone who does'. And then there is the evidence to back it up. The most commonly cited research on this side of the debate is a study carried out by Rindy Anderson and her colleagues, reported in an academic journal article titled 'Vocal Fry May Undermine the Success of Young Women in the Labor Market' from 2014.[25] They conducted an experiment in which 800 people were asked to listen to speakers aged 19–30 saying the phrase 'Thank you for considering me for this opportunity'. Each participant was faced with seven pairs of recordings, and they had to decide which one of each pair they felt sounded more educated, more competent, more trustworthy, and more attractive, before finally deciding which speaker they would hire. The difference between each pair of recordings was that one was allegedly displaying vocal fry and the other wasn't. Crucially, however, each individual pair of recordings was produced by the same speaker — one in their regular voice, and the other adopting vocal fry. The results quite clearly show that the voices with vocal fry were judged more negatively on every aspect than the 'normal' speaking voices, and that women were judged more negatively than men. You can't argue with that, it's science.

However, there are issues with the study. Rather than creating an effective matched guise test, in this experiment it was clear that each pair of voices were two recordings of the same person — one where they are using their normal voice, and one where they are using a lot of vocal fry. And not very convincingly.[26] It's hard not to suspect that the speakers weren't given much guidance and support when it came to producing authentic vocal fry, especially when we consider that throughout the article the authors themselves describe vocal fry as a vocal 'affectation'. As a result, all we can really deduce from the research is that when faced with young speakers who put on bad and exaggerated imitations of vocal fry in a job interview situation, people will judge them more negatively than if they were simply speaking in their everyday voice. I could have told them that. Although, even if the research was more robust and the speech samples used were natural examples of vocal fry, meaning that we could have a bit more confidence in the findings, the results would have probably been the same. People perceive vocal fry negatively, especially when younger women use it. But does that mean that we should encourage young women to adjust the way they speak and consciously avoid vocal fry? Short answer: no. Longer answer: no, why the hell should they?

Think about everything we have looked at so far about the way we speak being linked to who we are. Why should vocal fry be any different? This is the way these young women speak, and it is part of them. Why should they change it simply because somebody finds it 'annoying', especially when the same people will not find the same speech feature annoying when it is used by someone else. Vocal fry is just another way in which we are able to criticise and police women (especially younger women) on the basis of some made up rules. Which makes the numerous articles, news items, and blog posts urging women to change the way they speak in order to succeed no better than similar articles telling them how to look or how to dress. They are providing a solution to a problem that only exists because they have helped to create it in the first place. Such attitudes are at best, sexist, and at worst misogynistic. Change how you listen, don't ask people to change how they speak.

I mentioned uptalk earlier, where people go up in pitch at the end of a sentence, as if they are asking a question. The combination of vocal fry and uptalk is often pejoratively labelled 'valley girl' talk, originally used to describe a particular stereotype of young Californian women from the San Fernando Valley area, but later used to refer to any stereotypically materialistic and airheaded young woman. If you weren't aware of vocal fry before reading this book, I'm pretty sure you were aware of uptalk (or 'upspeak', or 'high rising terminal', or 'questioning intonation'). It has been a staple of speech criticism and mockery for years, with jokes usually based around not understanding why this person is making everything into a question.[27] Because yes, this is another speech feature for which young women are disproportionately singled out for criticism, despite men using it just as much or more in some cases (a good example of an uptalking man is George W. Bush).[28] But here, there are no mitigating circumstances around usual voice pitch making it more noticeable in women than men. This is simply a case of men and women using exactly the same speech feature, but being judged differently for it. When a young woman uses uptalk, she is perceived to be uncertain, tentative, and less intelligent. When an older man uses uptalk he is perceived to be in control — powerfully holding the floor in a conversation by making it clear he hasn't finished speaking yet and so not allowing the other person their turn.

Obviously, context plays a vital role in this — if a person is clearly in a position of relative power in a given context, then we are more likely to interpret their speech as powerful, and if another person is in a position of relative weakness, then we are more likely to interpret their speech as less powerful. But then this is precisely the issue — men, especially older men, are far more likely to hold positions of power than younger women, and so any evaluation of speech patterns is made against that backdrop of inequality. Young women are criticised for uptalk and vocal fry because they are young women, not because there is anything inherently negative about the speech features.

Do I sound gay?

In the documentary *Do I Sound Gay?* stereotypes about 'gay voice' are explored in some depth, as are people's feelings towards them. Several of the people interviewed recollect being bullied in childhood because of the way they spoke, and it is clear that some, even as adults, still feel as though they are being judged negatively at times. And because this kind of prejudice or stereotyping is based on voice, the very fact of whether an individual is or isn't actually gay ceases to be important — it's the perception of sexuality that is central. One of the people in the film, Chris, has this 'gay voice' despite being straight. He knows he gets perceived in a certain way, and he tells us that when he's on the phone he gets mistaken for a woman '98 per cent of the time' (which in itself suggests some interesting things about how certain speech features are seen as shared by women and gay men). Although, such mis-categorisation doesn't seem to affect him in a negative way. As Chris says: 'In the end, if someone thinks I'm gay, they're wrong. And there's nothing wrong with that.'

While Chris is not among them, many gay men do face prejudice when they speak. Among other things, this has been tied to the extent to which people believe we have control over the way we speak. A recent study by some psychologists at the University of Surrey found that straight people who believed it was possible to tell a person's sexual orientation from their voice and that gay people can control how gay they sound displayed stronger negative attitudes towards gay people.[29] Incidentally, the study also showed that straight participants believed it was much easier to tell a man's sexual orientation from their voice than it was to tell a woman's. This study explores what are known as essentialist beliefs about people's sexual orientation — the belief that there are certain characteristics shared by people of the same sexual orientation that are fundamental to their identity. In this case, the characteristic is speech.

So, what's going on? If we're saying that we all have some control over the way we speak, and also that men with gay-sounding voices will face prejudice, then why don't those men simply choose not to sound that way? Once again, the obvious response is 'Why should they?' This is part of who someone is, and is a mechanism for signalling that aspect of themselves along with a sense of shared group identity. Why should one group of people change the way they speak simply because another group of people doesn't like it? Or, to put it more honestly, why should one group of people change the way they speak just because another group of people doesn't like the particular combination of these speech features and this gender? Because if men with gay sounding voices are deemed offensive, and given that certain features of gay men's speech are seen as effeminate and shared by women, then surely these people must find women's speech equally offensive. Actually, maybe they do. Maybe we should all just learn to sound like stereotypical heterosexual men. That wouldn't be dull at all.

If we put voices aside for a minute, we know that LGBTQ+ people can face discrimination in the workplace, and a study carried out in 2005 in the US demonstrated how this can begin even at the point of recruitment. Sociologist András Tilcsik sent out fictitious applications to job advertisements in seven different states. For each advertised post, he sent two CVs a couple of days apart.[30] The CVs were different, but matched in terms of the candidate's qualifications, experience, and apparent suitability for the role. However, one CV in each pair included something that would suggest the applicant was gay, for example a role in a gay community organisation. He found that while the apparently straight applicants had an 11.5 per cent chance of being invited for an interview, the apparently gay applicants only had a 7.2 per cent chance. If people are being discriminated against simply due to the fact that employers think they might be gay on the basis of their CV, it's not difficult to imagine further discrimination happening on the basis of some people 'sounding' gay.

Not quite white enough

Consider the ease with which accent can be used as a way of excluding particular people from particular jobs or from housing opportunities, or even as a way of determining guilt in a crime. In the UK, the 2010 Equality Act identifies nine protected characteristics, making it illegal to discriminate against someone on the basis of age, disability, gender reassignment, marriage and civil partnership, pregnancy and maternity, race, religion or belief, sex, and sexual orientation. However, there is no section that prohibits discrimination on the basis of accent as such. As a result, somebody could be rejected for a job working in sales or on a reception desk because, 'customers might not understand them', or 'their accent doesn't match the image the company is trying to project'. In an interview in 2013, the entrepreneur and venture capitalist Paul Graham was talking about how his company decides which ideas to fund. Among other things he said: 'One quality that's a really bad indication is a CEO with a strong foreign accent. I'm not sure why. It could be that there are a bunch of subtle things entrepreneurs have to communicate and can't if you have a strong accent. Or, it could be that anyone with half a brain would realize you're going to be more successful if you speak idiomatic English, so they must just be clueless if they haven't gotten rid of their strong accent.'[31] Following a backlash, he later clarified that he was talking about the importance of being understood. When meeting potential partners and investors, he said, 'They're not going to work to understand you. So you can't make it be work to understand you.'[32] Common sense perhaps, right up to the point where you question why it is always the speaker that has to make the changes. Why can't we just get better at listening?

Because in the workplace, is it *really* the accent that is the problem? Is the person *really* hard to understand, or is their accent simply not white enough, or not English enough, or not home counties enough? And is it *really* the accent that doesn't match the company image, or is it that the speaker is too working-class, or too Black or too gay, or too trans? When it comes to issues relating to race and ethnicity specifically, there are a number of pieces of research that uncover some disturbing attitudes and practices.

The linguist John Baugh has researched and written about what is known as linguistic profiling, which is the same as racial profiling — the act of discriminating against a person on the basis of their ethnicity — only based on someone's voice. Baugh has written and spoken publicly about his own experiences of racial profiling, as well as inadvertent preferential linguistic profiling, as an African American man.[33] He talks about trying to rent a house for his family in California, where he was due to move for work. He describes how he would speak on the phone to prospective landlords using his 'professional voice' and arrange a viewing, only to then be turned down on a number of occasions when arriving at the appointment in person. Suspecting that the appointment was made on the basis of him sounding white on the phone (preferential linguistic profiling) and the housing was refused on the basis of him being Black in person (discriminatory racial profiling), he set out to explore the issue in more depth.

His subsequent work with two other researchers, Thomas Purnell and William Idsardi, demonstrated two important things.[34] Firstly, they showed that speakers of Standard American English, African American English, and Chicano English were indeed treated differently by prospective landlords in terms of the success in securing viewing appointments over the phone. They did this by using the matched guise technique, with tri-dialectal Baugh himself providing the voices (they also ran another experiment where Baugh's voices were played alongside other 'authentic' speakers of the three dialects, and listeners couldn't tell the difference). Baugh phoned each landlord three times, using a different voice each time, and starting each conversation with the same scripted phrase. Interestingly, his success in getting an appointment was strongly related to the existing racial and ethnic makeup of the geographical area, with traditionally white areas showing the strongest bias against both African American English and Chicano English enquirers with far fewer appointments made. However, when he used his 'white' Standard American English voice, his success rate was fairly stable across all regions.

The other important finding from a different part of the research was that people were consistently able to distinguish between Standard American English, African American English, and Chicano English, purely on the basis of the one word 'hello'. This would suggest that just as the attitudes that lead to racial profiling are triggered as soon as someone sets eyes on a person, the attitudes that lead to linguistic profiling are triggered equally quickly.

An updated version of this research was recently carried out by the linguist Kelly Wright, who found similar evidence of linguistic profiling, this time in relation to African American Language (equivalent to African American English described above), Southern American, and Mainstream US English (equivalent to Standard American English described above) in the housing rental context in Tennessee.[35] In describing the findings of her study, Wright makes an extremely relevant point in relation to the discrimination she uncovered. In her study she was the one calling the property managers to discuss renting the properties, so it was *her* voice(s) that were being judged in different ways. On this she says, 'Regardless of these differences I am one woman, with one larynx, one history, and one soul who was working to project courteous and confident professionalism in each call to property managers, regardless of voice used.' She goes on to explain that it is not her personal character that changes with each voice she uses, rather it is the attitudes that are activated in the listeners' minds by each of the voices. It's the listeners who ascribe different characteristics to each voice — characteristics which simply can't all be real, as the voices are coming from the same person.

Incredibly, we don't always need to hear different voices in order to negatively judge one speaker over another. I know this sounds confusing, but it relates to a famous study carried out by Donald Rubin in 1992.[36] He presented groups of students with part of a recorded lecture to listen to, while a photograph of the person apparently giving the lecture was projected onto a screen. The students then had to rate the speaker on various attributes, one of which was to do with whether the speaker had a 'foreign' accent. The thing is, while all the students were played a recording made by the same white American speaker from Ohio, not all the students were presented with the same photograph. Half of the students were given a picture of a white woman as the speaker, and the other half were given a picture of a Chinese woman. Incredibly, this affected the judgement scores relating to accent, with students who saw the Chinese face rating the speaker has having a more noticeable 'foreign' accent. In other words, their belief that they were listening to someone who was Chinese in origin actually caused them to hear an accent that wasn't there! Rubin and another colleague Okim Kang, refer to this as 'reverse linguistic stereotyping'.[37]

It's always about more than language

So, what does all this tell us about people's negative attitudes towards the way other people speak? Put simply, criticism about language is always about more than language itself. What it's really about is social class, gender, race, and all the other areas we've discussed. It's about one person or group of people feeling superior to another person or group of people, and finding ways to remind them of that perceived imbalance. Wherever we look we can see examples of language being used to create, reinforce, and maintain barriers between different sections of society. When comments are made about particular ways of speaking, they go much deeper than simply observing and evaluating a collection of sounds. They are comments on people's very identity, their sense of who they are. When you dismiss this or that regional accent as sounding lazy, or unintelligent, or untrustworthy, you are judging an entire group of people you have never met. And if you are a person with the accent that is being dismissed, you are aware that this is a comment not only on you and your accent, but also on your family and friends. When you pick out a particular speech feature for comment or ridicule, not only are you belittling the speaker, but you are belittling whatever social group they are part of.

Stories of prejudice

If you're someone who has never been criticised for the way you speak, you might be surprised at how common it is. During my research, I came across countless trainee teachers who had been told that their accent is 'too common' (although one teacher was told she was too posh and needed to 'rough up' the way she spoke); that they would be holding the children back if they didn't adjust it, that they should try to sound more like people from the local area (in this case the South East of England); or that they should make an effort to change a particular pronunciation. One teacher described being taken aside for a quiet word in the same way someone might be alerted about a hygiene issue. Another described their mentor's surprise at his decision to use his native Geordie accent to read a Thomas Hardy poem to the class.

Many of these were one-off comments, yet they have stuck in the individuals' minds for many years. And that's hardly surprising. Being told that 'you will make a perfectly adequate teacher, you just need to take some elocution lessons' is never going to do a great deal for one's confidence as a trainee teacher. But for some, the criticism has been constant. I spoke to an Australian teacher who lives in the UK, and she described the continual battle she faces over the way she speaks and how she is perceived as a result. She told me that for a while she deliberately moderated her Australian accent in order to fit in, but then hated herself for doing it, for hiding that crucial part of her identity. Now she simply bites her tongue when she's introduced to school visitors with, 'And here's our Australian; you might not understand what she says.' She told me that a 'posh' school she applied to work at actually mentioned that she drops her 'g's in the feedback as a reason for not giving her the job. And now she's tired. She's tired from having to constantly monitor her speech in order to match the expectations of those around her. She's tired from her life feeling like a continual performance, and that she can't be herself in a job she loves. And she's tired from the realisation that her accent now doesn't fit anywhere. She's always been cast as the outsider Australian in England, yet the repeated adjustments to her accent mean that she no longer sounds like the community of people she grew up with in Australia.

And it's not just teachers who are under pressure to change their accents — the kids can be too. In 2013, children at a primary school in Middlesborough were sent home with a list of words, phrases, and pronunciations that they were no longer allowed to use. These included well-known 'non-standard' phrases such as 'I done that', as well as more local accent features such as 'letta' and 'betta' (for *letter* and *better*). I'm sure the intentions were good, but such an approach has wider implications. You're basically telling the children that the way they speak, and the way their mum speaks, and the way their grandad speaks, and in fact the way almost everyone around them speaks isn't good enough. But against what criteria?

Because regional and socioeconomic background isn't a protected characteristic under the Equality Act 2010 in the UK, or under US and Australian law, our best source of information on language-based prejudice against regional and working-class accents is anecdotal.[38] The Accentism Project (Accentism.org) was set up in 2018 to collect stories of everyday prejudice and negative stereotyping, submitted by individuals who have experienced such things.[39] The idea behind it was twofold — to give people the opportunity to share their experiences and realise they are not alone, and to provide a body of evidence to support the fact that this is a genuine issue. Stories are submitted anonymously via the website and tagged according to topic. Visitors to the site can then browse all the stories, or search for specific keywords and find stories relating to those particular areas. The site also acts as a resource for people wanting to know more about accent discrimination, with links to media stories and academic articles. Below are just two of the many stories that have been collected.

> I am an undergraduate at the University of Oxford. I have a strong accent, as I come from Bradford. Since arriving at university, where the vast majority of people's voices ring with the supposedly dulcet tones of RP, I have constantly experienced problems due to my accent. I have been asked to 'speak properly' by tutors when speaking in tutorials. I have been mocked by other students due to my pronunciation of certain words. I have been told that I will never get a job if I do not allow my accent to 'mellow'- i.e. conform. In a progress meeting with tutors, I was told that my presenting skills needed work. I am a confident and skilled presenter: they just couldn't understand or wouldn't try to understand my accent.

> I was at a coffee machine and the man in front said I could go first as he was retired and didn't have to go

to work. He then asked what I did for a living... I said I'm an English teacher and he roared with laughter and said 'A Scouser....teaching English!!...they've got no chance!'

There's a lot to unpack in both stories. Accent and presentation skills are not inextricably linked. It's really not hard, especially during 2020 and 2021, a period which saw regular updates on the Covid situation from certain UK politicians, to find examples of RP speakers who are woefully inept presenters. In the second story we see a particular accent not being seen as appropriate for a particular role. Imagine! A teacher with a Liverpool accent! Whatever next? A national newsreader with a Birmingham accent?! Often, comments such as these are dismissed as trivial, or a bit of fun. But why should they be?

These experiences increase the expectation that such discrimination will take place, which in itself limits people's opportunities. A 2021 survey in the UK identified potential discrimination on the basis of accent as being something which concerned people who were looking for work (the top concerns were age, appearance, and disability).[40] Anxiety concerning the possibility of discrimination results in people not wanting to put themselves forward for roles that they feel don't suit their way of speaking. And even if that belief were to be unfounded, it would be enough to prevent that person from ever finding out, perhaps from reaching their full potential, and from challenging the status quo.[41]

The way that a lot of organisations address the possibility that people might be discriminated against on the basis of the way they speak, as well as the other characteristics such as age, gender, disability, race, and ethnicity, is to provide unconscious bias training to their staff. Such training centres on uncovering and reflecting on the preconceptions about some groups of people that we all have and which we might not be fully aware of. Unsurprisingly, the effectiveness of this kind of training seems to be mixed, depending on how seriously it is taken and how meaningfully it is both delivered and engaged with. But there is no doubt that the concept is valuable insofar as such bias does exist.[42] As far as I'm aware, accent is not something that is routinely incorporated into unconscious bias training, but it is starting to appear here and there.[43] In many ways it's a prime candidate for well-implemented training and awareness raising, as it is one of those areas where people often don't realise the strength or implications of their feelings towards some ways of speaking, be that to do with regional or national accents, or simply ways of speaking that are more commonly used by particular groups of people.

The fact is, it's very easy for language-related comments to be used as a proxy for other kinds of discrimination. Most people know that to suggest someone is unsuitable for a particular role on the basis of their gender, race, ethnicity, or social class is unacceptable. However, by convincing themselves and others that they objectively dislike people using 'swimmin'' instead of 'swimming', or vocal fry, or features of African American English, people are able to hide their class-, gender-, and race-based prejudices beneath a cloak of respectability. But the more we educate ourselves about this process, the more threadbare that cloak becomes. Because at the end of the day, accent prejudice is simply a way of laundering other prejudices into a socially acceptable format.

Ooh, he sounds like a baddie!

One area of particular interest when it comes to attitudes around accents is how they are used in drama. If you've ever watched the original 1994 film *The Lion King*, you may have wondered why Mufasa and Scar have such different accents, given that they are supposed to be brothers who have grown up together. Mufasa, voiced by James Earl Jones, has a rich, deep mainstream American accent, while Scar, voiced by Jeremy Irons, has a noticeable RP-like English accent. Admittedly, accent authenticity may not be your primary concern in terms of realism in this case, given that we are talking about a group of talking, animated animals, but the allocation of accent to character has not been made by chance. Put simply, Mufasa has a mainstream American accent because he is a 'good' character and Scar has an RP English accent because he is a 'bad' character. The filmmakers are leaning on stereotypes as a shortcut to represent particular character traits. In this instance, they are relying on an enduring stereotype within US films especially, which associates British English accents, and RP in particular, with refined, articulate evil.

This is not to say that British/RP-accented characters are always bad, or that mainstream American-accented characters are always good, but there is a pattern, and the idea of an RP-speaking villain has definitely been commonplace for a long time both inside and outside the world of Disney animation. Think of James Mason as Phillip Vandamm in *North by Northwest*, Ian McDiarmid as Palpatine in the *Star Wars* films, Tom Hiddleston as Loki in *Thor*, Angelina Jolie in *Maleficent* to name just a few. Perhaps this cliché will start to disappear as new productions introduce more diverse characterisations, but too many British-accented villains have been fixed on film for us to expect it to disappear any time soon. Certain stereotypes are so ingrained, filmmakers will continue to use them as cinematic shorthand despite their clichéd nature. Now, while the connection between RP and villainy might not be a particularly damaging stereotype in wider society, other often-used accent and character pairings are a lot more problematic. For example, low-status, foolish, and often dishonest characters in US animated films are frequently given African American or Hispanic accents. Watch the hyenas in *The Lion King*, or 'The Amigos' penguins in *Happy Feet*, for example. The character of 'Eduardo' in *Despicable Me 2* is just one big bundle of lazy, stereotypical Mexican clichés. That these stereotypes are repeated across many films is no coincidence; these are conscious decisions that filmmakers take — good, positive, or socially attractive characters are more likely to have mainstream/standard 'native' accents and dialects and bad, negative, or socially excluded characters are more likely to have non-standard or 'foreign' accents and dialects. If you have ever watched a James Bond film you will be aware of clichéd movie villains and their dubious accents. I noticed recently that on the 'Eastern European' section of a website belonging to an established voice actor agency they acknowledge that 'Eastern European and Russian accents seem to be the preferred choice for video game bad guys and movie villains made for Western audiences' (likely reflecting Cold War enmities) — and the fact that these stereotypes also exist in films aimed at children is a cause for concern.

Linguist Rosina Lippi-Green identifies this issue in her book *English with an Accent*. She makes the point that 'children are not passive vessels who sit in front of the TV and let stories float by them. What they take in is processed and added to the story of data on how things and people are categorised.'[44]

Lippi-Green draws on her own detailed research into the use of voice in animated Disney films to paint a rather bleak picture of how language-related stereotypes are used. She studied 38 full-length films (24 in detail in 1997 and a further 14 in less detail in 2010) made between 1937 and 2009, observing the linguistic choices made in relation to each character. Among her findings she discovered that in the 24 films from her first study there was a clear bias in terms of the relationship between accent and character motivation. Whereas around 20 per cent of the 'standard' US English speakers are bad characters, this proportion doubles to around 40 per cent for 'non-native' English speakers. Not a consistent distinction by any means, but certainly a tendency.

Lippi-Green also explores the representation of African Americans in Disney's animated films, both in terms of the African characters being portrayed and the Black actors behind those portrayals. Once again, the original *The Lion King* proves to be of interest, primarily because of the inconsistency between context, casting, and character along racial lines. We have already discussed the disparate accents of Mufasa (African American actor) and Scar (white English actor), but it is the main character, Simba, son of Mufasa and future King, who Lippi-Green pays particular attention to. Both young Simba and adult Simba are played by white American actors (Jonathan Taylor Thomas and Matthew Broderick respectively, although young Simba's singing was provided by Jason Weaver who is African American) using mainstream US English. Given that Simba's mother, Sarabi is played by a Black actor (Jamaican-born Madge Sinclair, albeit again using a mainstream US accent), Lippi-Green asks why Prince Simba, African son of African characters played by Black actors, in a story set in Africa, is played by white American actors.

Now, you may well ask that once the decision has been made that these three related characters (Mufasa, Sarabi, and Simba) are all to use pretty much mainstream US English anyway, why should the race and ethnicity of the actors matter, especially as these are animated characters? That would be a reasonable question if it weren't for the fact that elsewhere in the film, for example in the case of the hyenas, African American English *is* used to help create a character, and the actor providing the voice is Black American (Whoopi Goldberg playing the cunning and sadistic Shenzi). This reinforces the idea that while Black actors are able to use African American English in the film, its use is reserved for when the accent fulfils the stereotypical requirements of characterisation.

The Lion King is a great example of the process we're discussing, and there has been a lot written about it, but you can find similar examples elsewhere.[45] In addition, you could look at films where accent is being used creatively, such as *The Death of Stalin*, set in Soviet Russian in 1953. In this 2017 film, director Armando Iannucci made the conscious decision to have actors use a variety of British/US accents rather than all adopt a faux-Russian accent (the technique often used to indicate another language in an English-language film). Iannucci has since explained that using Russian accents would have sounded too artificial and would have killed the comedy of the film. He also makes the interesting point that Russia, being the size it is, has a huge variety of accents, so to have all the actors using a uniform version of 'a Russian accent' does this variation a disservice.[46] Perhaps the most striking accent (even more so than Stalin's cockney and Krushchev's Brooklyn) is the strong Yorkshire accent spoken by war hero Georgy Zhukov, played by Jason Isaacs.[47] Not a Yorkshire native himself, Isaacs described his decision to use that accent in the following way:

'In real life, Zhukov was the only person who was able to speak bluntly to Stalin. So, I thought, well, who are the bluntest people I've ever met in my life? They're all from Yorkshire. The accent is shorthand for: no fucking around, I'm going to tell you what's what.'[48]

It's an interesting take for a Russian character, but still plays into well-worn tropes in terms of British regional accents.

Even if you aren't yet quite on board with the potential harm such stereotypes can and do cause in our day-to-day lives outside of film and TV, it is impossible to deny that accent is indeed regularly used as a way of creating character, or that this characterisation relies heavily on pre-existing stereotypes. And you can see why film and TV producers do it — it's quick and efficient. How else can they immediately let the audience know that this character is educated, or a gangster, a joker, or someone untrustworthy? How can they show that this person is likely to align with a certain viewpoint, are likely to have this social or ethnic background, a particular political loyalty, or sexuality? Sure, they could use up valuable time with action and dialogue that will explain each person's character, connections, and allegiances, or they can simply have them say a line in such a way that demonstrates all of that.

It's possible to explore the same processes and techniques at play in a much more parochial setting. For example, in the long-running BBC radio drama *The Archers*, a programme that has been on air since 1951 and is reported to have an average listening audience of around five million. It is set in the fictional county of Borsetshire, and centres on the lives of the residents of Ambridge, a typical English rural village with farming at its heart.

In some ways radio drama is even more interesting than film and TV with regard to exploring how characters are created, due to the fact that it has fewer resources at its disposal to help with the characterisation process. In film and TV a character can be dressed in a certain way, can move in a certain way, and the camera can observe them in a certain way, all of which helps to define a character before a word is even spoken. Radio drama has none of this, so relies much more heavily on speech. Of course, *what* a character says will have a great bearing on how they are perceived, but *how* they say it is just as important.

The most obvious way in which accent is used in *The Archers* is to help create broad social class distinctions. There are very clear social divisions within the community of Ambridge, particularly with regard to the landowners and the land-workers. Characters at the top of the social scale, such as Brian Aldridge, speak in predictably 'posh'-sounding RP-like accents, while people at the bottom, such as the Grundy family, have distinctly 'rural' ways of speaking. In between these extremes, there is a tendency for the less serious and often comical characters such as Tracy Horrobin to have more markedly 'regional' accents (even if those accents are not always from the apparent local area), and the more serious and 'successful' characters such as Jim Lloyd have more RP-like accents. Then there are other familiar tropes such as the cockney wide-boy Matt Crawford and the RP uber-villain, Rob Titchener.

> The Grundys' rural accent brings us to an interesting point. Because *The Archers* is set in the fictional county of Borsetshire and has an uncertain geography, there are limited clues as to what a 'local' rural accent might sound like. As a result, characters such as the Grundys tend to display some quite generic 'rural England' linguistic features. For example, the vowel in words such as *mind* sounds a bit like 'moind', the vowel in words such as *shop* sounds a bit like 'sharp' (but without

the 'r' being pronounced) and the vowel in words such as *trap* is elongated. There is evidence of rhoticity, which means there is a clear pronunciation of 'r' at the end of words such as *tractor* and in words such as *farm*. Combined, these features serve the purpose of generating a stereotypical 'rural' sound in the minds of the listeners, even though it isn't in fact an identifiable regional accent.

The linguist Jane Hodson, in her book *Dialect in Film and Literature*, makes an interesting distinction between character stereotyping and linguistic stereotyping. Most of what we've looked at so far comes under character stereotyping — the representation of particular groups of people as having particular characteristics. Yes, the groups have been identified in part through their use of language, but that language is a means to a (stereotypical) end. Linguistic stereotyping, on the other hand, shifts the focus onto the language itself and explores the extent to which an accent is an accurate portrayal of how this accent is actually used, or is itself a clichéd and narrow stereotype. Clearly, the two go hand in hand in creating and reinforcing the overall stereotype, but it does add insult to injury when the accent itself is not even realistic. In the case of the Grundys, I would argue that there is an element of linguistic stereotyping fuelling the character stereotyping. A generous interpretation would be that the actors and producers are specifically aiming to create a non-specific but hopefully inoffensive 'rural' accent by drawing on known features from other rural English accents. That these features are employed inconsistently and sometimes inaccurately (the best example of this is a rhotic 'r' where none exists, for example at the end of the names *Emma* and *Mia*) is just one of the programme's charms. A less generous interpretation is that the actors were told to 'sound rural' and then each character proceeded to draw on every clichéd feature at their disposal, regardless of whether it makes any linguistic sense.

But are we reading too much into all of this? Film, TV, and radio drama are fictional representations of the world — why should they be one hundred per cent accurate in their portrayal? And if character stereotypes do exist in film, TV, and radio, aren't they simply reflecting those that already exist in wider society? Otherwise, how would they work?

With regard to film and TV not being 'real'. If these dramatic representations don't exist in the real world, where do they exist? Yes, the worlds created within the drama might be modified versions of ours or completely made up, but the representations themselves (the films, programmes, and books) exist in our 'real' world alongside the rest of us. When we watch a film, that film becomes part of our life experience in a similar way to when we observe or interact with people on the street, or in a shop, or at work. In fact, if we don't have access in our day-to-day lives to people from different cultures and social backgrounds, it might well be that our exposure to them in film, TV, and radio is the only information we have on which to base our knowledge. So yes, in that sense these representations do matter.

These stereotypes do already exist in wider society, so you could say they are simply reflecting what is already there rather than creating anything new. However, stereotypes only continue to be relevant by being repeated and reinforced, and this is the role being played by film, TV, and radio. This ties into the point above about the (lack of) distinction between the 'real' world and the worlds being created in the drama. While it might suit us to think of the real world and the worlds being created in drama as being entirely separate, they simply aren't — they undeniably feed off one another.

By the way, it's only fair to warn you that when you start to become more aware of the ways in which accent is used in drama, especially the lazy and negative ways, you start to notice it everywhere. You begin to second-guess the casting, directorial and actors' decisions in everything you watch, wondering whether an accent choice is intentional, and if so, what was the thinking behind it? Personally, I don't see this as a bad thing, as it's all part of becoming more aware of how language works. But you might want to wait until the film's ended to start talking to your family about it.

That's not for you to use

I actually have a bit of experience when it comes to voicing unpopular linguistic opinions. Every now and then, I get asked to comment on a language-related story in the media. I think it's fair to say that most people actually have quite conservative views when it comes to language matters. A lot of people do honestly think that standards of English are slipping and that some ways of speaking are objectively better than others, and they don't take too kindly to smug, bearded, bald academics coming on the TV and radio to tell them otherwise. And these people certainly don't like it when such academics suggest that their views on accents could, in actual fact, be seen as discriminatory. This is what happened in the summer of 2021 when I was invited to a televised debate to discuss accents and stereotypes.

The news story that initially sparked the debate involved the owner of an Italian restaurant who had complained on social media about how some customers think it's acceptable to imitate an Italian accent when they speak to him, in a way that he feels is mocking. This was then picked up by the popular morning news and current affairs programme *Good Morning Britain* (*GMB*), who thought they might use it as the basis of a wider discussion about whether it is ever socially acceptable to mimic 'foreign' accents.

A few days before the debate, one of the producers called me to ask how I felt about the issue. I explained that, to me, imitating people's accents is indeed problematic. When it comes to imitating accents associated with different languages and cultures, people should ask themselves why it is that some accents are seen as acceptable to mimic while others are not. For example, would the people who imitated an Italian accent in a restaurant do the same in an Indian restaurant, or a Chinese restaurant? Probably not. What about a French restaurant, or a Turkish restaurant, or a Greek restaurant? Or what about if they had a Dutch colleague at work — would they imitate their accent? Possibly. But what about a Nigerian colleague, or a Korean colleague? I explained that in my opinion, the very fact that someone might have to think whether mimicking this particular accent is or isn't offensive is quite a good indication that it probably is, and that you probably shouldn't.

But what about mimicking regional accents? Again, I explained, this is potentially problematic. When people use a specific accent when telling a story or a joke, it is usually because there is an association between that accent and a particular social stereotype. They might be trying to get across that the person is unintelligent, untrustworthy, over-confident, or mean and will use a voice (and accent) that helps portray this. And this isn't a neutral decision. The speaker will choose an accent, whether consciously or unconsciously, that they believe will help portray the relevant characteristics that will make the joke or story work. And the only way this will be successful is if the listener has a shared understanding of the association between the accent and the stereotype.

Having satisfied the producer that my comments would generate the required amount of discussion and outrage, a date and time for the *GMB* debate was arranged. I was told that the other person in the debate would be an actor who felt that there was no real harm in mimicking people's accents, and that we should all just get a thicker skin. The producer also told me that due to some technical difficulties in previous programmes, they would send a camera operator to my house, rather than rely on Zoom or Skype.

On the day, the camera operator arrived, and we set up in my back garden. He got the camera and microphone ready, tested it was all working, then we chatted about his favourite and least favourite accents, and how many languages I speak (one)[49] while waiting for our time slot. I double-checked I was only in shot from the chest up, to ensure I was safe in my decision to dress for business upstairs and holiday downstairs (TV-ready shirt and smart jacket accompanied by scruffy shorts and trainers) then I was connected to the studio via my earpiece, and we were ready to go. I couldn't see the person I was debating with, I could just hear them in my ear, so for the next ten minutes I had the strange experience of sitting in my garden on a beautiful July morning, looking into a TV camera while having a conversation with the people in my ear, as neighbours walking their dogs wondered what was going on.

The debate itself went well, and I managed to say most of the things I had wanted to. Although the other person and the presenters disagreed with me, it was a nice enough conversation, and an interesting way to spend ten minutes before the day job. The way I view all these things is that having the discussion out there is generally a good thing, and even if just a few people take a moment to reflect on their attitudes towards language, that is still a positive outcome.

Debate over and camera packed away, I went back to work to a series of online meetings. It was only when I went to make a cup of tea a bit later that somebody brought my attention to a story on the *Daily Mail* website. For non-UK readers, the *Daily Mail* is usually described as a right-wing tabloid and has a reputation for sensationalist stories. The article in question had the headline '"This bloke is destroying British humour": *GMB* viewers mock linguist who claims mimicking a foreign accent is as offensive as using blackface'.[50] Underneath was a not especially flattering still of me from the TV interview followed by an account of the debate. The whole article was illustrated by tweets criticising my stance. The quote in the headline was itself from a tweet that read, 'The British sense of humour is being destroyed by this bloke. Imagine actually knowing him. That must be a real nightmare', to which both of my daughters replied, 'actually he's not a nightmare, he's our dad, so back off' or words to that effect. Love those girls. I then went on Twitter myself to have a look at what else was being said under the hashtag #GMB. And sure enough, there were lots and lots of tweets pointing out how wrong I was, how I didn't know what I was talking about, and how people should just toughen up and not be so offended. There were a few tweets that supported my opinion, but they were in the minority. The comments made on the article itself were (and still are — they remain visible for all to see) even worse. They take aim at my opinions, my university, my credentials as an academic, and even my appearance! There were 380 comments in all, when I last looked, and while I haven't read all of them, the vast majority disagree with what I said, often in very strong terms.

Many of the tweets and comments picked up on the

question of comedy in film and TV, which had been a fairly small part of the discussion, but which was given prominence by the headline of the story in the *Daily Mail*, and some of the references used to illustrate it, such as Basil Fawlty and Manuel from the TV series *Fawlty Towers*. Somebody suggested I need to 'grow up and watch some episodes of *It Ain't Half Hot Mum*', a 1970s British TV series now known for its racist, homophobic, and imperialistic themes. The TV comedy angle is interesting, as it's an area where accents traditionally play a huge role, perhaps even more so than in film and other areas of TV. Decades and decades of TV and radio comedy shows have routinely relied on the use of regional and foreign accents to help make their jokes, sketches, and situations funny, as have thousands of stand-up comedians, and millions of everyday people trying to make their friends laugh. Practices have undoubtedly changed over the years — where it was once completely acceptable to have people in blackface, brownface, or yellowface and using grotesquely clichéd accents to match, this is now, fortunately, much more unusual. Even *The Simpsons* was quite recently forced to realise that having a white actor voice the clichéd Indian shopkeeper Apu was problematic.[51] However, same-country regional accents, and foreign accents where there isn't such an obvious historical imbalance of power and prejudice, are still fair game.

Now, despite what the *Daily Mail* might think, I am not on a quest to destroy British comedy by policing accents. Neither am I suggesting people should not be free to use an accent that is not their own when recounting some anecdote or other. And I am certainly not arguing that actors shouldn't be using different accents in their various roles. However, what I am saying is that we should all at the very least be reflecting on how accents are used, both by us and by others. If you work in film, TV, radio drama, or if you're a comedian, is this really how this character needs to speak? And even for the rest of us, is this really what Dave from the pub sounds like, or is this just my over-the-top 'northern' accent? Does Kasia from the office really speak like a 1960s East German spy from the movies, or will this little story still work if I use my own voice?

Even as I write this, I can imagine the groans of annoyance as some of you start to wonder who the hell this bloke thinks he is, telling us to 'reflect on our use of accents' when you're in the privacy of your own home; has he not heard my Latvian butcher joke? To be fair, even my own family had something to say after the GMB debate, with my wife commenting, 'I presume this means you're going to stop imitating your kids' Bolton accents now?' Fair point. And I will — as long as they stop taking the mickey out of my Hertfordshire one.

I would like to bring up one last point on accents in comedy, as I've just had a painful flashback to something that happened in 1993. I used to work as a TV extra (if we ever meet, just ask me who was the first police officer on the scene when Trevor Jordache's body was found under the patio in *Brookside*). Once, I worked for a couple of days on *The Russ Abbott Show*, a comedy sketch show based around the comedian Russ Abbott and his various characters. Most of the time, the extras were there to be in the background of the sketches while the main action happened — just regular passers-by. But I knew that for one of the scenes I was supposed to be a cowboy. As the scene approached, one of the assistant directors came over to tell me I had a line in the cowboy scene, and was that okay? Obviously this was okay, as a line meant extra money. 'Oh, and we need you to put on an American accent, as the scene is set in the old Wild West.' Hmm. I was then taken away to have my makeup done and the scene was explained to me. It would open with Russ (we worked in TV together, I can call him Russ) crouching by a river, apparently panning for gold. Then I was to swagger in, see him, and in my best Wild-West accent say, 'Hey there old-timer, are you looking to find some gold?' To which he would reply with something along the lines of, 'I will be, just as soon as I find my contact lens.' (I didn't say the programme was actually funny, just that it was a comedy.) Cue canned laughter. We did the scene without too many problems. Well, I say 'we' but the way things work in TV is that they often only use one camera, so we do the scene with the camera pointing at Russ while I deliver my line off-camera, and then they turn the camera to point to me and we do it all again. By the time it was my turn to be filmed, Russ was off getting changed for the next sketch, so I'm just saying my line to precisely nobody. But anyway, job done, I went home, happy with my extra pay, and confident that none of my student friends would see my appalling attempt at the accent.

A few weeks later, the TV was on in the background at our student house, when suddenly I heard my voice saying, 'Hey there old-timer…' followed by the whole sketch, then an announcer saying, 'This Thursday at 7.00, *The Russ Abbott Show*!' They were using my sketch as a trail for the programme! All week. Several times a day. So I think you'll find, *Daily Mail* readers, that far from destroying British comedy, I actually played a pivotal role in the success of UK accent-based humour in the mid-1990s.

So what do we do?

Faced with all these negative attitudes, prejudices, and potential discrimination, what can we actually do about it? You might well read all this and use it as evidence and reassurance that you were right to change your own accent or dialect, get rid of your vocal fry, sound 'less gay', teach your kids to speak 'properly', or encourage the use of Standard English and even RP in schools, as this is how people get ahead in society given the status attached to speaking a certain way. Because this does leave us with a familiar challenge. It's all very well for me, a white, educated, middle-aged man, to say that people shouldn't change the way they speak simply to appease those who are judging them from their thrones of inequality, but this is the reality that people face. If someone finds themselves in a situation where they are likely to miss out on an opportunity purely because the people who are giving them that opportunity have narrow views about a particular way of speaking, then the temptation is obviously to adapt. If you dress a certain way for an interview, why not speak in a certain way? Of course we act differently in specific situations — if we are someone who tends to swear a lot, we will probably show restraint in a more formal context, so why can't we stop using uptalk, or vocal fry, or glottal stops?

Again, it's an example of the inequality that exists. I imagine that almost anyone would be viewed somewhat negatively in a formal interview situation if they turned up wearing old jeans and a t-shirt and kept swearing, when everyone else was dressed smartly and kept their language clean (whether or not this *should* be how interviews happen is a different discussion, but for now, let's just acknowledge that this is the case). But only *some* people would then be viewed negatively for using, for example, uptalk and vocal fry.

I can't for a minute argue with the logic of wanting to change the way you speak as far as it relates to your own specific context. However, what I would fight against is the system that allows and maintains that inequality to thrive. I understand why people might think they should teach their children to speak in a certain way, in a way which asks them to reject some of what makes them who they are, but I just can't help thinking we should be doing more to build a society in which that kind of sacrifice isn't necessary in the first place.

CHAPTER 4

Style-shifting and code-switching: why does Mum sound so posh on the phone?

In the middle of the 2022 campaign for the leadership of the UK Conservative Party (and, therefore, the next prime minister), Scottish rapper and social commentator Darren McGarvey made the following observation:

'You've got a country of tens of millions of people being taught to "speak properly", to accommodate the inferior communication skills of privately educated people who can only speak to people who speak like them. They think they're cultured? I can go to a recovery meeting and speak to a heroin addict then on to a corporate or political event then go home and talk to my wife and daughter. That's changing through about five different gears in a 12-hour period. How many gears has Rishi Sunak got? Who's truly cultured there?'[1]

Far from being something to be ashamed of, adjusting the way we speak is a sign of effective communication. But the extent to which you do it (or feel you have to do it) depends on the world, or worlds, you inhabit. Because people often feel uneasy when they notice others changing the way they naturally speak, despite the fact that we all do it to some extent or another (yes, even you). The technical term for this is style-shifting (you will also hear it referred to as code-switching, but I will explain the difference shortly) and it is an entirely natural feature of spoken language. It describes the process of adjusting the way we speak according to context, such as the well-known phenomenon of 'phone voice', when your mum goes from shouting at you because of the state of your bedroom to using her posh phone voice to answer a call, all in the space of ten seconds. Style-shifting is a way of projecting subtly different identities depending on where we are, who we are with, what we are trying to achieve, and the extent to which we want either to fit in or to distance ourselves from particular people, groups, or situations. We might even shift our style as a result of how much we like the person we are speaking to, and how much we want them to feel towards us. We actually learn how to adjust our speech very early in our lives. If you have children, just think how their speech changes when they want something from you!

Shifting terminology

This kind of adjustment is referred to as code-switching as well as style-shifting. Some linguists tend to use the terms one way, other linguists use them another, and normal people use whichever term makes most sense to them once they are aware there is a name for it (and their choice can sometimes tell us something interesting about how they view the process, as we shall see). But I think it's worth separating the two here. Put simply, it makes sense to think of code-switching as moving between two different languages, and style-shifting as moving between styles within the same language. This is how I will use the terms here, unless referring to someone else's work where they are used differently.

If you are fluent in more than one language you will sometimes switch between languages in the course of a conversation, especially if you are around people who are equally linguistically able. You might switch to accommodate the understanding of whoever you talking to (your mother-in-law's English is good, but she doesn't know the phrase *tea cosy*, for example). It could be that a particular word comes to you more quickly in one language than the other, or that a particular phrase is more appropriate in one language than the other, or it might be that certain emotions or topics feel more naturally expressed in one language than the other. This is code-switching. Style-shifting, on the other hand, describes the situation where we stay in the same language, but adjust the way we are using it. Perhaps we use more or less 'formal' words and phrases, perhaps we adjust our pronunciation, perhaps we add or remove slang or swear words. It can be useful to think of style-shifting as movement within and between repertoires, where a repertoire refers to a collection of speech features that are available to us in a given context.

> You can actually illustrate style-shifting to yourself in a simple way if you like. Take a feature that is known for being quite variable, such as 'f' for 'th', 'in' for 'ing', or a glottal stop for 't', and think about which of the two options you usually use. Then simply try to use the other one more. Say something now to try it out, such as: *I'm thinking of changing the way I speak but I'm not sure if this accent is best. I'll try it for three months and see how I'm getting on.* First say it how you would usually say it, then, if you usually pronounce some of your 't's

as glottal stops, make a point of saying them all as clear 't's (in *not, accent, best, it, getting*). Or if you usually pronounce them as 't's, try using a glottal stop. For the 'ing' words (*thinking, changing, getting*) try alternating between 'ing' and 'in'. And for the 'th' words (*thinking, three, months*) try using 'th' or 'f'. The temptation is to overdo it and start adding all sorts of other features in to emphasise what you might see as especially 'posh' speech or 'lazy' speech, but even if you manage to just change those individual sounds, you will definitely hear a difference.

Some situations are clearly either code-switching or style-shifting. For example, a Bengali-English bilingual moving between English and Bengali over the course of a conversation with their equally bilingual friends is code-switching, and a receptionist interrupting a chat with a colleague in English to answer the phone using their professional voice (also in English) is style-shifting. However, not all contexts fit so neatly into the two categories. For example, what about a speaker who moves between African American English (AAE) and White Mainstream English (a term coined by April Baker-Bell to emphasise the racial element of American English and that the perceived 'standard' version is rooted in white ways of speaking and writing). Or between traditional Yorkshire dialect and 'standard' English? Is that style-shifting or code-switching? At what point does a difference of dialect become a difference of language? This is actually a well-known question in linguistics — how do we determine precisely what a language is, and how do we distinguish one from another? On the surface, this seems like an easy issue to deal with, and we can provide endless examples of two clearly different languages (German and Mandarin, Danish and Urdu, Arabic and Swahili, and so on). But languages have fuzzy edges — they are not clearly defined and can't always be easily distinguished from one another. When we take two completely different languages, such as Mandarin and French, we don't need to worry about the edges. But what about Danish, Swedish, and Norwegian? These languages are so closely related that they could be thought of as dialects of the same language. It's not the case that everyone within the three countries can understand each other, and some aspects overlap more than others (Norwegian and Danish share more vocabulary, while Norwegian and Swedish share more pronunciation), but generally, there is a level of mutual intelligibility. So why do we think of them as languages and not dialects? The answer is political — they are different countries with their own national identities, and so they have different languages.

In China, people speak different varieties of the Chinese language that are actually mutually unintelligible. Even speakers of some of the main varieties such as Mandarin, Cantonese, and Wu are not able to understand each other, yet these varieties are referred to as dialects within China. The reason is that China is a single nation, and so it makes sense from a sociopolitical perspective to put forward a picture of linguistic unity. Linguistically, the main varieties found in China are closer to languages than dialects, and the varieties found in Denmark, Sweden, and Norway are closer to dialects than languages, but politically they are seen as the opposite. You may have heard the famous saying 'A language is a dialect with an army and a navy', usually attributed to the linguist Max Weinreich, but actually a recollection of his hearing it elsewhere.[2] This neatly sums up the non-linguistic motivation for labelling languages, particularly neighbouring languages. It is much more to do with the organisation of people than it is to do with language itself.

Knowing this, we can actually learn a lot by observing how speakers themselves refer to what they do. If a linguistically aware (as in, they are conscious of adjusting their language and have reflected on the process) African American English speaker sees their manoeuvring between AAE and a 'standard' or 'mainstream' variety as code-switching rather than style-shifting, then that actually tells us something interesting about the way they view the differences between the two ways of speaking. It suggests that they see it as something more than simply speaking the same language in a different way, which then has likely implications for how they see themselves and others when they are using each variety. It suggests that it is not only their use of a particular variety that relates to their identity, but it is also how they view those different varieties that are available to them.

Style-shifting, which will be the main focus here as this is a book primarily on English, is generally described in three ways, each focusing on a different influence behind the adjustment. Firstly, there is 'attention to speech', which was originally proposed by the linguist William Labov.[3] He noticed that people tend to use more standard features when they are in situations in which they are paying more attention to their language. It sounds obvious in some ways, but Labov was one of the first to test the idea methodically. It accounts for the fact that if we are reading something aloud to a group of people, we are likely to pay much more attention to how we are pronouncing the words than if we were simply chatting to a friend, and so orient more towards what we see as a more 'correct' way of speaking.

The second way of looking at style-shifting is in relation to the 'audience design model' described by the linguist Allan Bell, which suggests that the adjustments we make are influenced primarily by our 'audience', who we are speaking to at any particular time.[4] According to this idea, we adapt the way we speak in order to sound more or less like the people around us, depending on how we feel towards them. What also matters is their role in the conversation — are we speaking directly to them, are they part of a wider group, are there eavesdroppers listening in? The way I always visualise this is by imagining an awkward office party where people are standing around drinking warm wine from plastic cups and trying to have a good time. Some people will be talking in groups, some people will be talking in pairs, some people will be standing quietly alone, and some people will be holding court to a group of people who would rather be somewhere else. Everyone is very aware of who can hear what they are saying, and you can guarantee that some people look like they are talking to one group of people, but are really speaking extra loud so as to 'perform' to the wider group. Perhaps it's to impress the boss (perhaps it *is* the boss), perhaps it's to get the attention of a co-worker, but whatever it is, they are adjusting their speech as a reaction to their audience, and that audience might not be the obvious one in front of them (who are simply wondering why this person is speaking so loudly). There are similarities between this and the idea of attention to speech, in that context influences the way we speak, but the audience design model focuses more on our awareness of the people around us rather than on the language itself.

The third way of looking at style-shifting is in relation to a 'speaker design model', whereby we use our stylistic shifts as ways of demonstrating our attitudes to what is being said by others, as ways of shaping interpersonal relationships, and even as ways of constructing and performing our individual identities. It suggests that the way we speak helps us to create who we are in a particular context. The extent to which we are doing this because we want to, or because we feel we have to for fear of being judged, or something worse, depends on the situation. This speaker design approach doesn't mean that the other two ways of looking at style-shifting — attention to speech and audience design — are wrong, it simply means that there is more to it. In reality, style-shifting is likely to be a combination of all of these things. We adjust the way we speak depending on the formality of what it is we are saying, which is related to our audience at that particular time, which is in turn related to the identity we want to put forward.

Everyday chameleons

I've spoken to some people who, when asked, 'Do you ever change the way you speak?' will answer with a straightforward, 'No, never. This is the way I speak, take it or leave it.' And while this might be true to a degree, it is unlikely that they really do maintain precisely the same way of speaking in every situation. I mean, maybe their romantic partners, while in the throes of passion, get the same linguistic treatment as the cold-caller attempting to sell an extended warranty, but somehow I doubt it. I wonder if, for these people, there is a sense that style-shifting is a sign of weakness, of not being true to yourself or trying to be someone you're not. A few years ago, I met Andy Burnham, who, as I write this, is the Mayor of Greater Manchester, and has been since 2017. He kindly took part in research we did in 2016, which involved getting into the back of our Accent Van (a mobile recording studio) and answering some questions about the way he spoke and how it related to the local area.[5] Andy is an interesting case because he grew up in Liverpool, but was at the time an MP in Greater Manchester, and there can be quite a fierce rivalry between the two areas. When asked about his accent, he said:

> I get criticised by people in the media at times who claim I put on a northern accent, or if I'm in Liverpool, play up the scouse, turn down the Manchester, or in Manchester do the opposite and play up the Manchester side of my accent. The truth is I've got a generic northern accent and I wouldn't want to change it. It's who I am. I think if you start changing the way you speak, you quickly get into difficulties as it sounds like you're trying to pretend to be someone you're not, and in my profession, a politician, that's not a great thing to do.

I wonder if he was thinking about George Osborne's mockney?

Awkward chameleons

Shifting between the subtly (or not so subtly) different versions of 'you' at home, at work, with friends, and with the delivery driver will probably be so routine as to be unnoticeable for many people. But when you find yourself in a less familiar situation, especially one in which there is a mismatch between how you perceive yourself and how others perceive you, then things can get a bit trickier. You can see it in young people especially, as they negotiate their various emerging identities in the world. For example, you might have a teenager, let's call him Harry, who has two distinct groups of friends — one from school and one from an outside hobby: music — and he is a slightly different person in each group. Perhaps he is especially loud and a bit sweary in the school group, but in the music context he is more reserved and polite; two identities which emerge, in part, through speech. This is fine until the two groups meet at a party, at which point Harry faces a bit of a dilemma — does he maintain his school identity and risk his music friends seeing him in a different light, or does he maintain his music identity and risk alienating himself from his school friends? Another fascinating situation of this type is when young people unexpectedly bump into a teacher outside of school (to be fair, this can be an equally awkward encounter for the teacher, especially as the kids get older and the social contexts start to overlap more) — do they continue with their non-school identity, or do they feel the need to switch back to their school way of acting and speaking? You might get to see this a little bit if you're a parent or carer and your kids are at a school where you all go to parents' evening together. I'll never fail to be amazed at the ability of one of my children, at parents' evening, to switch from slightly stroppy teenager to model pupil in the time it took to walk through the hall and sit down at the next teacher's desk.

Most of us face situations where we feel uncomfortable about how we are (or how we might be) perceived. This might be related to social class or social background, it might be related to some other perceived social grouping such as gender, ethnicity, or sexuality, or it might just be to do with professional background and experience. When we find ourselves in those situations where we stand out for whatever reason, we can suddenly become a lot more aware of how we speak.

For me, the awkwardness comes from a mixture of regional accent and social class. As you know, I come from Hertfordshire in the south-east of England, but I live in Bolton in the north-west of England. And as we've already discussed, there is a perception that a southern English accent can stereotypically sound 'posh' to northern English ears. Add to this the fact that I come from a typically British middle-class background, I have to face the fact that I can indeed sound a bit posh to some people. I don't think I sound posh; I sound the same as most of the other people I grew up with, who also don't think they sound posh. But I know enough about language to be able to see that yes, my accent is objectively closer to an RP accent with all its inherited prestige than it is to a typical Bolton accent. So sometimes, when I find myself in a situation where I'm talking to everyday people with everyday Bolton accents, I will suddenly be acutely aware of how I sound and will start panicking about whether people are thinking: 'Who invited the posh bloke?' The feeling is at its worst when someone has come to my house to do some work such as replacing the boiler, or fixing the roof (i.e. a 'proper' job), and we end up having a chat about work. He (it's usually a he, so let's throw a bit of sad masculine inadequacy in here too) will undoubtedly ask what I do for a living, at which point I start the awkward explanation of what linguistics is, and what a professor of sociolinguistics actually does. Don't get me wrong, I usually love describing my job and explaining why I think it's vital that we all know more about how language works, but I generally need a bit of time to get into my stride. Give me a room full of prospective students and parents on a university open day and within fifteen minutes I've got them seeing the benefits of studying linguistics. But when I'm shouting up to a bloke on a ladder, my explanation loses a bit of its persuasive nuance, and my answer to 'How many languages do you speak, then?' (still one) always disappoints.

But more important than what I'm saying is what accent I use. Yes, I'm painfully aware of sounding posh in this situation, and I don't like it, but should I change it? If so, how? I can't suddenly adopt a Bolton accent! So, what do I do? Reflecting back on my many years of having people fix things in my house in Bolton, I can tell you that the answer is I move to anywhere between slightly less posh to some kind of a weird cockney stereotype (to gain covert prestige, where a non-standard accent carries social power). So much so that on one occasion my wife popped her head around the door to see why Danny Dyer was in the kitchen distracting the man fixing the washing machine. At that point it's better if I just don't say anything.[6]

But I'm not complaining. Not for a second. My 'posh' voice creates problems for me in a tiny minority of social situations. And when we say problems, we are talking minor social awkwardness at worst. On the other hand, it has allowed me to enter spaces of education, employment, and even broadcasting without even a hint of accent self-doubt. I have always known my accent will fit those contexts without even raising an eyebrow, purely because it happens to match a historical and social idea of prestige. That is a privilege that I only became fully aware of when I began to study how language works. And that is a privilege that I am attempting to challenge from within, partly by writing this book.

Serious switching

For many people who don't experience the same kind of privilege I do, code-switching or style-shifting can be a mechanism for survival. In a fascinating BBC Radio documentary *Code-Switching*, Lucrece Grehoua speaks to young Black people in Britain about their experiences of changing the way they speak.[7] Each person she interviews relates their way of speaking to who they are, often reflecting on how exhausting it is to consciously have to change and monitor such a vital part of themselves in their day-to-day lives. Whether it's pronouncing words in a certain way, or raising the pitch of their voices, or otherwise acting and speaking 'white', they talk about all the additional things they have to consider simply to get along in a world that is balanced in favour of people who don't look or sound like them.

One of the people whose experiences resonated most for me is Leon, now a barrister, but who learned to code-switch (this is the term used in the documentary and commonly within Black communities, so I will keep it here, although it could be classified as style-shifting) to get where he wanted to be. He mentors young Black men and is insistent on teaching them the necessity of code-switching for their own safety, especially when dealing with the police. In the documentary he recounts a story from his 20s where he was stopped and searched by armed police and explains how code-switching was his way of managing what was clearly a volatile situation. He says:

> If I had reacted in a way that was what they deemed aggressive, if I had put more bass in my voice, if I had moved my arms around, that could have been the difference between walking away free or being shot, in my opinion.

He then shares the advice he gives young people about the importance of being aware of, and managing, people's preconceptions:

> That's what I say to all young Black men — in those circumstances, when people are looking at you for a particular bias or stereotype anyway, do not give them a reason to act upon that stereotype or bias. Because if they do it can result in your death.'

If you're reading this book as someone who has only ever had to adjust the way they speak in order to move between the, let's face it, very safe identities of parent, employee (especially if most people speak in the same way as us anyway), friend, or customer, then it is probably worth taking a moment to reflect on the realities of Leon's life and those of the young Black men he supports. Imagine being in a situation where you fear for your life, knowing that doing nothing more than speaking the way you naturally do will put you in mortal danger.

The kind of code-switching described by Lucrece Grehoua and the other contributors is a fact of life for many people whose way of speaking doesn't fit the linguistic norms of majority-white spaces. As a result, changing the way they speak is something that gets drilled into young people of colour from a young age. At home, *learn to speak properly if you want to stay safe*; at school, *learn to speak properly if you want to succeed* ... Good advice. Or is it? Perhaps a different lesson might be: *learn to speak appropriately in any given situation*. In other words, style-shift (or code-switch). This way we are less likely to belittle someone's everyday way of speaking, we are instead acknowledging that it might not be suitable for some situations, such as in the classroom, or in a job interview, or in the workplace, so it is more advantageous to learn to speak in a way that matches people's expectations in those contexts. You can still use your other way of speaking, but better to keep that for at home or with friends.

But is this really any better? Who decides what is or isn't appropriate for a given situation? While such an approach doesn't explicitly say that this way of speaking is right and that way of speaking is wrong, there can be no question that it places different ways of speaking at different levels and assigns them different social values. It might come from a well-meaning place, but teaching young people that they have to style-shift/ code-switch if they want to succeed in life is reinforcing the idea that their way of speaking (and therefore their way of being, and their sense of who they are) is not good enough. We can convince ourselves that we are simply preparing young people for the realities of life, but that isn't going to change the underlying problem, especially when that problem is rooted in historical racial inequality. In fact, some would argue that any small superficial benefits a person gains when they practise style-shifting/code-switching are actually outweighed by the harm to their sense of self and mental health that can be the consequence.

One such person is the teacher, researcher, and activist April Baker-Bell. Baker-Bell is the author of a powerful book called *Linguistic Justice: Black Language, Literacy, Identity, and Pedagogy*, which aims to challenge and dismantle anti-Black linguistic racism and white linguistic supremacy in the US education system.[8] She sees code switching as a mechanism by which young people are sacrificing their Black culture and identity in favour of a white middle-class identity. And who can argue with that? We've already seen how a so-called Standard English emerges not through any inherent superior quality, but rather through it being the language of those in power. And in the US, the power imbalance between middle-class white and working-class Black Americans is vast. We've also seen how incredibly close the relationship can be between how we speak and who we are. So how can the adoption of White Mainstream English by a young Black American who grew up with African American English (or, using Baker-Bell's deliberate term, 'Black English') be seen as anything but an (at least partial) adoption or imitation of a white middle-class identity?

Linguist Rosina Lippi-Green, author of *English with an Accent*, wrote the following:

> We do not, cannot under our laws ask a person to change the color of their skin, her religion, her gender, her sexual identity, but we regularly demand of people that they suppress or deny the most effective way they have of situating themselves socially in the world.[9]

This sums the issue up very effectively, both in the US and the UK context. Compared to 50 years ago, we are (generally) more aware and tolerant of differences in religion, race, ethnicity, gender, and sexuality. But we are still telling children that this way of speaking is better than that way of speaking if you want to be accepted and succeed in the real world. How is it different to saying, 'Look, it's ok to be gay, Muslim, trans, or Black in your own time at home and with friends, but it's probably best to just be a bit more, erm "conventional" when you start work.'?

But what about situations like those described by Leon earlier in which he felt his life was actually in danger if he didn't adjust the way he spoke to the armed police officers? Can we really advocate not code-switching? Baker-Bell has a powerful message on this point in the context of the US. She explained how the Black students she worked with in Detroit questioned the effectiveness of code-switching to White Mainstream English in the face of discrimination. And they had some convincing evidence: young Black people are still being killed by police even when they use Standard English. Which leads Baker-Bell to ask, 'If using white mainstream English cannot protect Black people from losing their lives, why are we telling Black children that code-switching is a strategy for survival?'[10]

Few people would question someone's effort to do whatever they felt was necessary to defuse or to stay alive in a given situation. Few people would question a teacher coaching a young person to speak a certain way for an upcoming college interview.

But we need to open our eyes to the bigger picture. We need to be critically aware of the social context in which this is happening, and the inequalities that make it necessary. If we are going to teach young people to style-shift or code-switch, we need to do so in a context where we are at the same time challenging the systems that demand they do so. We need to make sure young people are aware of what they are gaining and what they are sacrificing by agreeing to change the way they speak in order to fit in with mainstream society and its expectations. It will always be their decision, but it is on us to make sure they understand all of this and can make informed choices. We should also remember that the people who are going through school now are the very same people who will be employing future generations and running our various schools, businesses, societies, and countries. If we want to break the cycle of linguistic superiority and standard language ideology, then this is probably a good place to start.

Shifting in action

One of my favourite academic studies into style-shifting (I know, we all pretend not to have a favourite, but there we are) is a piece of work carried out by the linguist Devyani Sharma,[11] and a follow-up piece she did with Ben Rampton.[12] Sharma was interested in the ways in which people from the Indian community in West London shifted between different accents in their spoken English. She had the sense that people tended to speak in more of a 'British accented' English or more of an 'Indian accented' English depending on the contexts they found themselves in. To explore this, she and her colleagues asked some participants to record themselves as they went about their day-to-day lives, talking to different people. They then listened to the recordings and, for each speaker, noted how often a particular sound was pronounced in a more British way, and how many times it was pronounced in a more Indian way, and when each pronunciation was more likely.

> To give you an idea of what this might sound like, let's look at a couple of these sounds that vary. One is what's called a retroflex 't', which I mentioned in Chapter 2. This is where the 't' sound is produced with the end of the tongue curled backwards as it touches the roof of your mouth when you make the 't' sound. For the purposes of this study, this is the Indian-accented way. Another sound that they focused on was the 'l' sound at the ends of words such as *cool*. In most British English accents, we have two quite different pronunciations of 'l', what we call a 'clear' or 'light' 'l' and what we call a 'dark' 'l'. You can hear (and feel) the difference between them quite easily. First, say the word *like*, but pause as you are saying the 'l'. Listen to that sound and feel where your tongue is. Notice how the tip of your tongue is touching the roof of your mouth just behind your top teeth. This is a clear 'l'. Now say the word *pill* and pause again on the 'l'. The sound should be different, and you should notice that your tongue is in a different position. Now, there is a bit more of your tongue touching the roof of your mouth rather than just the tip. This is a dark 'l'. While British English has these two options, Indian accented English will tend to only have the clear 'l', so when a word such as *feel* was pronounced with a clear 'l' in the study, this was seen as the Indian-accented way.

Sharma and her colleagues listened out for these differences in the pronunciation of 't' and 'l', along with some other sounds which also vary, and started counting to see how often they were used and in which situations.

One of the clearest examples of somebody adjusting their speech between British-accented and Indian-accented English was a 41-year-old man called Anwar. He showed a great deal of variation in speech styles, and it seemed to depend on who he was speaking to. When he was talking to a Sri-Lankan maid, he used almost 100 per cent Indian features, but when he was speaking to a car mechanic who had a cockney accent, he used almost 100 per cent British features. Sharma also noted several contexts in between, where Anwar would use a mixture of features, sometimes using more Indian than British, and sometimes using more British than Indian. Perhaps Anwar uses these subtle adjustments as a way of performing, or at least foregrounding, his British or his Indian identities at different times.

But then things became even more interesting. In the follow-up study, Sharma and Rampton started to look not just at how someone's speech varies according to context, but how someone's speech can vary within the same conversation with the same person! They analysed a conversation between Anwar and Sharma about a time Anwar had visited a museum, dividing the conversation into chunks, and once again counting the examples of British or Indian pronunciations. They were then able to work out the proportion of British-English pronunciations in each chunk and see how that proportion changed over the course of the conversation. They noticed that at some points in the conversation Anwar sounded particularly British and used only British features, and at other times he sounded particularly Indian and used only Indian features. But here's the fascinating part. When they looked even more closely, Sharma and Rampton found that these changes in pronunciation aligned with changes in the topic of the conversation. The points of the conversation at which Anwar was using the most Indian pronunciations were the same points at which he was recounting Britain's role in the turmoil of India's past and expressing his dismay at the injustice of British museums displaying what are widely regarded as stolen artefacts. Sharma and Rampton interpreted this as Anwar using specifically Indian pronunciations when he is expressing 'personal or political outrage' or 'cultural insult'.[13] In other words, Anwar was using particular linguistic features as a way of aligning himself with particular cultural viewpoints and identities as the conversation unfolded. Anwar had two distinct ways of speaking available to him, and both were clearly 'his' to use. Would anyone question his use of either British or Indian English as he navigated his social world?

Authenticity

This is a good time to discuss how free we are to adopt various ways of speaking, or whether all speech features are available to be used by all speakers. This relates closely to the question of how things are interpreted, and once again underlines the importance of context. On a practical level we can say that anybody can use any pronunciation they choose, albeit with a bit of practice. There aren't any sounds in any varieties of English that are impossible to learn for other English speakers. It is true that we are all constrained in some ways by the speech sounds we grew up with, and it is also true that the ability to fully acquire a different accent (be that from a different language or within the same language) decreases when we reach adulthood, but if we really wanted to, we could learn the sounds of other accents. However, on a social level, there are limitations as to what different people can use, especially if the aim is to be understood in certain ways. We know of the stereotypical connections between some accents and particular characteristics such as 'friendliness' and 'intelligence', but does that mean anybody can simply slip into a Boston, an Edinburgh, or a Multicultural London English (MLE) accent in order to temporarily acquire or project those associated personality traits? Could a British prime minister, on reading opinion polls suggesting they were coming across as unfriendly, suddenly decide to adopt a Geordie accent in order to exude a new approachability? Could an elderly lady from Surrey slip into MLE to emphasise her toughness on the streets of Hinchley Wood? Could a white American teacher switch to African American English (AAE) in the classroom? They could try (and some politicians have), but it wouldn't really work. And in some cases, it would be blatantly racist. Language doesn't usually act alone, not in everyday life. It exists alongside our behaviour, our dress, our ethnicity, our social background, the context we are in at the time. It also exists alongside expectations of those around us. The reason a British prime minister is unlikely to suddenly adopt a Geordie accent is because we would know they don't habitually have one (no prime minister so far has anyway). The reason our elderly lady from Surrey is unlikely to be taken seriously if she adopts an MLE accent is because that style doesn't match everything else about her. The reason the white teacher shouldn't adopt AAE is simply because the language is not theirs to use. That's not to say that people don't routinely adjust the way they speak and even adopt a different accent, as we have seen, but when they do, and when the adjustment is conscious, the change is perhaps more likely to be in one direction — towards some kind of a perceived standard. People would be mocked (and are mocked, think back to Ocasio-Cortez and Osborne) if they were to suddenly adopt a Yorkshire accent or a Brooklyn accent in a white-collar workplace, yet nobody really questions people adopting RP, or mainstream American English, however far that might be from someone's original accent. Because these accents are 'proper', and the ones we should be aspiring to use, right?

Lose your accent, and you will succeed!

If we accept the fact that we all style-shift to an extent, and that we might feel the need, rightly or wrongly, to speak in a certain way in more formal situations, we may well wonder how to actually go about it. Fortunately for everyone (I am, of course, joking), the days of telling people they don't speak properly and then charging them to fix the problem are not over. 'Accent Reduction' is big business. There are numerous companies that promise to 'lessen' or even 'get rid of' the accent that they remind you is clearly holding you back in life. Often, the service is targeted at people who have a 'foreign' English accent, and who want to, or feel pressured to, make it sound more like that of a 'native' speaker. But it's also aimed at people who want to 'soften' their 'regional accent'. If you're interested in the inventive ways various companies try to frame their services so as to avoid saying 'we will teach you how to speak properly', just search online for accent reduction. It would make a lot more sense to set up a company that teaches people to listen more effectively, but I doubt there's the demand.

The problem with questioning the value of accent reduction services is that people do face real issues due to the way they speak, and they can't wait for society to move on and become more accepting — they have to address the issue themselves. So I won't criticise the people who seek out such services, or even all of the people who provide them. However, I will criticise the ways in which the services are often marketed, and the ways in which the industry as a whole justifies its existence.

Below are a few problematic phrases taken from the promotional material of various accent reduction specialists. Notice how they clearly frame the issue as a problem (yours) that has to be fixed (by them).

'We deal with all RP (received pronunciation) English sounds in this speech training manual, which will help you sound educated.'[14]

'How to get rid of a foreign accent in English: 5 easy steps.'[15]

'The first step to losing your accent is the desire and determination to improve your pronunciation with accent reduction coaching.'[16]

'You want to fit in, be heard, and get ahead, but your accent is holding you back.'[17]

'Don't let your foreign accent prevent you from achieving your dreams.'[18]

There's a big question mark over whether and why someone would want to aim for a 'native-speaker' accent in a second (or third, or fourth) language anyway. There's an assumption, which the existence of accent reduction services reinforces, that everybody's ultimate aim in learning and speaking a second language is to speak in a way that makes us indistinguishable from people who grew up speaking the language. While this might be true for some, it is not the case for all. A second language English speaker's quest for a more 'native' accent should not be viewed in the same way as Mick and Sue from down the road wanting to perfect their Italian pronunciation in time for summer in Tuscany. Many people learn English or another language (such as French) through necessity rather than explicit choice, and they might well be doing so against a backdrop of colonial, or other social inequality and even animosity. For people acquiring English in these situations, sounding like 'one of them' (often the colonisers and the oppressors) is not always a desirable aim, especially when they are already part of a clearly defined group based on a shared first language, race, and ethnicity. A piece of research carried out in 2005 explored this idea and suggested three possible strategies that people use to navigate allyship through pronunciation.[19] The first strategy is to attempt to achieve as high a level of proficiency in the second language as possible in order to gain access to the power and status of the other group. The second is to do the opposite and aim low in terms of proficiency, thus maintaining loyalty to one's own culture and distancing oneself from the new. The third is perhaps the most interesting, as it involves striving for as high a level of proficiency as possible while retaining and manipulating particular pronunciations that clearly demonstrate where one's loyalties ultimately lie. In other words, people deliberately keep hold of accent features from their first language, however proficient they are in the second language, as a way of demonstrating their first language (and associated national, racial, or ethnic) identity.

I found this same thing happening in my own research when I was looking at whether Polish people in Manchester acquired a Manchester accent. I noticed that some of my participants had a Polish-influenced 'k' at the end of 'ing' words such as *working* or *talking*. By looking at lots of other related factors, especially their stated future plans and their intention to stay and settle in Manchester or eventually move home to Poland, I came to the conclusion that they were using the feature more or less consciously as a way of signalling an allegiance or solidarity with their Polishness. In other words, despite probably being able to produce a more native-like pronunciation, their use of 'ink' was a small way in which they could display and perform their Polish identity.

The process of accent reduction is fundamentally flawed anyway. It is impossible to speak without an accent — all we are doing is replacing one accent with another. And this is more than simply making your accent objectively more 'understandable', the declared aim that gives the industry its legitimacy. Instead, it is buying into the idea that accent B is somehow better than accent A. If we then look at this from the perspective of identity, it raises some important questions — by changing people's accents, are we changing their identities? And what of the element of ethnicity? Is this process fundamentally racist?

It's certainly classist. George Bernard Shaw's play *Pygmalion* explores the idea of accent reduction within the same language. In it, Professor of phonetics Henry Higgins takes on the challenge of teaching 'common flower girl' Eliza Doolittle to speak properly, and thus be passed off as a duchess. The plot relies heavily on notions of social class, and the extent to which spoken language is tied up with our position in society. The play has some fun with the process of different aspects of speech being adjusted inconsistently, resulting, at one point, in Eliza's accent having become more refined but the content of what she says betraying her less cultured background. For example, in the middle of tea with some well-to-do guests during which she is trying so hard to use her new accent, she announces that her Aunt died of influenza, but that it was her belief that 'they done the old woman in'.

Although the play premiered in 1913, and the London of then is nothing like the London of now, the perceived need to speak 'properly' in order to better oneself is still very much alive. English accents have changed in the last 100 or so years, and Higgins' boast of being able to place a man within two miles or even two streets by the way he spoke would be a lot less believable now due to the linguistic diversity we enjoy, but the underlying point of the story remains valid. There is a widespread view in society at large that in order to get ahead, you must learn to speak in a certain way. It's impossible to overstate how pervasive this view still is.

One language, one nation, one ideology

Language is hugely important to nationhood. In fact, any definition of 'nation' will include a reference to a shared language. An extreme version of this results in what is often referred to as the 'one language, one nation' ideology: the belief that 'monolingualism or the use of one single common language is important for social harmony and national unity'.[20] This ideology has been articulated in various contexts in recent history relating to English. Here's US President Roosevelt in 1919:

> We have room for but one language here and that is the English language, for we intend to see that the crucible turns our people out as Americans, of

American nationality, and not as dwellers in a polyglot boarding-house.[21]

And British Prime Minister Johnson 100 years later in 2019:

> I want everybody who comes here and makes their lives here to be, and to feel, British — that's the most important thing — and to learn English. And too often there are parts of our country, parts of London and other cities as well, where English is not spoken by some people as their first language [incidentally, how does one change their 'first' language?] and that needs to be changed.[22]

And most recently, the current text on the website of the Australian government's Department of Home Affairs:

> People living in Australia should make an effort to learn English. It is important to learn to speak English because it helps to get an education, a job, and better integrate into the community. It is essential for economic participation and social cohesion. Australian society values the English language as the national language of Australia, and as an important unifying element of society.[23]

So, to paraphrase all three as a single question: why don't immigrants to these countries just make an effort and learn English? On the surface, it doesn't seem to be an unreasonable question. And you might well be thinking, 'If I decide to move to France I am absolutely going to make an effort to learn French in order to fit in — it's just common sense.' But would you be moving to France under the same conditions and for the same reasons that many people move to the UK, or to the US, or to Australia? If you were to choose to move to France, might you have far more time and far greater resources with which to learn French than the average migrant or refugee? Of course it is beneficial for immigrants to learn to use the language they will be surrounded by, whatever the context, but things simply aren't that straightforward. Learning a language is hard. And telling people they *must* speak English will not make it any less hard.[24] If it is important to the UK government that everyone learn English, they could properly fund classes that would help people do it. But unfortunately, in England at least, this is not policy. In Wales and Scotland it is; both countries have put such funding in place already. In fact, the Welsh government not only provides English language education, but also Welsh language tuition for asylum seekers who come to Wales. And, for the rest of the population, the Welsh government recently announced that they will provide free Welsh language classes to people aged 16–25 and all school teaching staff. Similarly, the Scottish government funds online resources to help people learn Scottish Gaelic. Yes, the statuses of English, Welsh, and Scottish Gaelic are different, but it's still good to see two governments doing this work well.

In fact, the continued use of Welsh in Wales is a good example of the relationship between language and national identity. Anyone who lives in or who has visited Wales will be familiar with its use of Welsh in various contexts, for example on its bilingual road signs. But this wasn't always the case. In 1536, the language was banned for use in public administration in favour of English. Then, in 1549, it was no longer to be used as the language of public worship. The Welsh language continued to decline over the next few centuries. It didn't disappear completely, and was still spoken by some as a first language in certain areas of the country, but it wasn't widely used. Its resurgence in recent years can be put down in part to the creation of a national Welsh language radio station and later a television channel, as well as various government acts that raised the status of Welsh to that of English in the public sector. In doing so, the Welsh Government made the link between the Welsh language and national identity explicit, claiming that 'it is an essential part of the cultural identity and character of Wales. It helps define who we are as a nation'.[25] It is this sense of identity that fuels this kind of reform and encourages people to keep a marginalised language alive. Understanding a national language such as Welsh allows people today to reconnect with their cultural history. It connects modern Welsh speakers with the writing, the culture, and the people of Wales's past. It helps provide an identity that relates to what has gone before. The same is true of any language, but it is especially strong when a people have been colonised and their language is under threat.

The ability to understand and speak Welsh in 2022 is a strong element of a Welsh identity, but it's not the only element — things are never that simple. There are plenty of non-Welsh speaking people in Wales who identify strongly as Welsh. (In fact, there was a recent documentary on BBC Radio 4 that explored this very issue, suggesting that the Welsh identities of non-Welsh speaking Welsh people were being devalued.)[26] Although, most people who speak Welsh do indeed identify as Welsh.[27] And then what about the incomers? My father-in-law lives in north Wales (an area where the position of the Welsh language has always been strong), having retired there over 20 years ago. He enrolled in Welsh language classes immediately after moving there, and has been a fluent Welsh speaker for years. Seeing him in action, I have absolutely no doubt that his Welsh is deployed at times strategically to distance himself from the rabble of English tourists that descend on his town in the holiday season. In those situations, he is Welsh. Just listen to him.

In Australia, there are ongoing discussions, concessions, and conflict around the status and role of Aboriginal languages. For First Nations here and elsewhere in the world, language is a core part of who they are, and a way of connecting with the shared cultures of the people that came before them. Those languages have been systematically devalued, marginalised, and even destroyed, and the impact is still felt deeply. In a report made for an Australian House of Representatives committee on the subject of language learning in First Nations communities, Yurranydjil Dhurrkay, a member of the Galiwin'ku community of what is now known as north-east Arnhem Land, was quoted as saying: 'Our language is like a pearl inside a shell. The shell is like the people that carry the language. If our language is taken away, then that would be like a pearl that is gone. We would be like an empty oyster shell.'[28] The monolingual, English-only parliament in the Northern Territories specifically barred Aboriginal languages from being used in its chambers, despite 70–100 per cent of the population in most non-urban areas speaking an Aboriginal language, and 42 per cent of the overall population speaking something other than English at home. Advocates for the inclusion of Aboriginal languages were not asking for everyone else to suddenly become familiar with them, they were simply asking for the use of interpreters — a process that works successfully in other parliaments, such as that of New Zealand. In July 2022, the Australian rugby union team hit the headlines by singing their national anthem in Yugambeh — an Aboriginal language from what is now known as south-east Queensland. Although praised in much of the mainstream media,[29] the reaction on social media was not all so positive.[30]

But if one nation must have one language, which version of that language must they use? When Boris Johnson was speaking about the necessity of people learning English, what English did he have in mind? It wasn't the English you'd hear in some of the deprived areas of the country far away from London, or the English spoken by people in Islamabad. Instead, it was the mythical and idealised standard that is unconsciously evoked when we use language labels. The definition of the word 'English' in relation to language might *technically* include all of the different accents, dialects and varieties that exist within the UK, USA, and around the world, but when it is used in the context of language learning or language policy, its meaning tends to be distilled into one particular (desirable) type of English. And so we return to the standard language ideology, where everything is neat and tidy with clear edges. But real language isn't like this, as becomes very clear when we start to look beyond the 'one nation, one language' monolingual ideal.

For many people it is perfectly normal to operate in two or more different languages on a daily basis. In fact, it is estimated that most people in the world speak more than one language, and it is their monolingual friends who are in the minority. Depending on your own background and geographic location this fact might be surprising or so obvious you are wondering why it is even being mentioned. Given that this book is written in English, if you are surprised at how widespread multilingualism is, it is a safe bet that English is your mother tongue, and that one of the reasons you aren't as familiar with the ability to speak multiple languages is that you have never needed to! English is often described as a 'world language', meaning that it is used by so-called native and non-native speakers alike in order to communicate globally. The result of this is that if you happen to acquire English as your first language growing up, the practical necessity of learning additional languages is far less than had you grown up using Xhosa, or Turkish, or Pashto.

The reasons behind English becoming a world language — largely colonisation, technology, and timing — and the reticence of first-language English speakers to acquire additional languages are the subject for another book. What we are interested in here is exploring how being multilingual, and able to operate across two or more languages, relates to who we are.

Multilingual chameleons

In many ways, the process of code-switching between languages and style-shifting within the same language is very similar. In both cases a speaker may consciously choose one variety or another based on who they are speaking to and the context they are in. The choices and changes can occur because of context or topic of conversation, and shifts can even occur just for the duration of a single word or phrase. The difference is that, unlike with same language style-shifting, switching between languages might make speech unintelligible to certain listeners. If we're thinking about how we can use language as a way of signalling group identity, what clearer way is there of achieving this than consciously making yourself understood by some people and not by others?

But before we launch into looking at how our choice of language interacts with our sense of identity, let's just revisit our terminology. The problem with the term code-switching is that it suggests a process of switching between two or more clearly defined languages, each with its own identifiable boundaries. But, as we've seen, languages simply don't have neat and tidy boundaries, and they certainly don't have neat and tidy boundaries when they are stored in our minds. Code-switching implies a situation where different languages are somehow stored separately from one another and that we can switch between this or that language (or temporarily dip into this or that language) as required. One situation requires us to activate Arabic and turn off English, while another situation requires us to activate English and turn off Arabic, for example. In this scenario it should be possible at any point to identify which language is being spoken at any particular moment in time.

But while code-switching can be a useful term with which to describe and analyse at which points the speakers shifted into which different languages and why, this isn't how most people experience multilingualism. For most people the different languages aren't stored nice and neatly in their own separate areas of the brain, ready to be activated and deactivated when the need arises. For most people the situation is a lot more fluid — they just have a whole lot of language up there. Sure, the different languages *tend* to stick roughly to their own area, with English over here and Italian over there, but languages are social – they like to mingle. Imagine planting three proliferating plants right next to each other (or maybe planting one or two, then adding another one later). One with bright green leaves, one with dark green leaves, and one with reddish leaves. As they grow, they will intertwine and overlap. It will still be possible to identify which plant is which, and it will still be possible to trace a particular branch or leaf back to its source plant, but in some places, all you will be able to see is a mixture of greens, or a mixture of greens and red. To make things more complicated, the two plants with green leaves are actually quite closely related, and their leaves are not always easy to distinguish. And of course, while all of the plants are potentially fast-growing, their actual performance will depend on the soil in which they all sit, the environment around them, and the attention each one is given. One might be deliberately nourished, while another might be somewhat neglected. That's more like how languages exist alongside one another.

This more mixed-up way of thinking about different languages is a better reflection of people's mixed-up ways of using languages. At times it might be relatively easy (and desirable) to mentally prioritise and access one language over another, perhaps when there is a clear divide between the language someone uses at work and the one they use at home. But at other times there simply isn't that need, especially when people are communicating with other multilinguals who share some or all of each other's languages. When we share multiple languages, it is much more likely that instead of rigidly sticking to one or another, we drift in between them to a greater or lesser extent.

When we start to think of language in a more fluid way, and when we start observing how people actually use language on a day-to-day basis, the term code-switching seems less appropriate. So, what else have we got? We can use 'code-mixing', which suggests that the languages or varieties being used can be combined. Or we can use the more recent term 'translanguaging'. I say recent, but these things are all relative — the term was originally used by a man called Cen Williams in the 1980s to describe the practice of using two languages (in this case Welsh and English) in the classroom.[31] But in the last 10–15 years it has been used more widely to describe multilingual interaction. From the outside, translanguaging isn't actually that different to code-switching or mixing — if we were observing them both, we would see people moving between languages in the course of an interaction. The difference lies in how it is viewed from the inside. In fact, what makes it a useful concept is precisely that it does take an insider perspective. When we describe code-switching, we start from the idea that there are two or more named languages or varieties being used, and then we look at how the speaker moves between them, alternating between features belonging to this language and features belonging to that language. However, when we describe translanguaging, we start by considering all the language the speaker has available to them, and then looking at how it is used, without the need to categorise features as belonging to this or that language. Instead, the features all belong to the speaker, as part of their own experience of language.[32]

The key element of translanguaging is challenging boundaries. Those boundaries might be the ones we construct between named languages such as English and Urdu, or they might be the ones we create between different types of communication such as linguistic and non-linguistic. In that sense, translanguaging is about going beyond the boundaries of what we see as 'language' altogether. As the linguist Li Wéi puts it, 'Language in its conventional sense of speech and writing is only one of many meaning- and sense-making resources that people use for everyday communication.'[33] Translanguaging is an attempt to accommodate this fact.

While we're in the process of describing new terms and making you think 'since when has that been a word?', I have one more for you. Along with some other linguists, Khawla Badwan, when describing the language use of multilinguals especially, is very keen on the term 'languaging'.[34] But this is more than just translanguaging without the 'trans'. Badwan uses languaging as a verb, meaning that we can start talking about it as something we do. Just as we walk, we work, and we sleep, we also language. It's a wonderfully inclusive way of thinking about how we all communicate, how we all draw on whatever linguistic and non-linguistic resources we have available to us (speaking, reading, writing, signing, and more), whether those exist across named languages or across varieties within the same named languages.

Despite having explained all this, for the purposes of this book I'm going to continue to use the term code-switching, simply because this is the term that most people are aware of, and it is sufficient for the scope of what we are exploring. However, I'm using it with the understanding that things are less rigid than the term might imply.

So, let's look at what code-switching actually entails from a practical point of view. Linguists often distinguish between 'situational code-switching' and 'metaphorical code-switching'. Situational code-switching is perhaps the more 'mechanical' of the two. It describes the type of switching that happens when something about the context of an interaction changes. For example, when a group of British people are in a café in Spain and are chatting among themselves in English, but then switch to Spanish when ordering their food (I know, I know, they are just as likely to simply say what they want in English, loudly, with a bit of a Spanish accent, but let's just imagine for a moment). Or when a group of people are speaking in one language, but then another person joins them who doesn't share that language, and so the conversation switches into a language they can all understand. The term can even be used to describe the experience of not knowing or momentarily not remembering a particular word for something in one language (maybe the word doesn't even exist in that language), and so using the equivalent word in another language. All of these instances of code-switching are quite functional, practical, and largely deliberate.

Metaphorical code-switching, on the other hand, is more than just a mechanical, functional shift between the two languages. Here the change can be seen as part of the process of expressing one's attitude or ideological stance towards the topic of conversation, to signal allegiance and solidarity towards something, or to distance oneself from something else. Crucially, it can be a way of indicating and even performing a particular identity. For some people, switching between languages can be like switching between personalities, for others it is less extreme. But it is hard to believe that there are no differences in our sense of self and our sense of how we are being perceived as we change the language we use, if only on the basis of the associations, friendships, and experiences that each language will bring to mind. It is not uncommon to hear people describe that they feel somehow different when using their different languages. Perhaps they feel more assertive in one language compared to another, or more laid-back, or more playful, or more aggressive. Such differences could be put down to the contexts in which each language has been learned and routinely used. If we learn German purely because we have a job in which our role is to negotiate with other German-speaking businesspeople, then our use of German is likely to be bound up with feelings of assertiveness and diplomacy. If we learn Tagalog because our partner is from the Philippines and we want to be able to communicate with their family, then our use of Tagalog would probably create very different associations.

Because of these associations, our use of different languages goes beyond the purely functional. In this case, Tagalog would become a safe, intimate, friendly language that we might slip into in conversations with our partner when expressing something particularly emotional, even when the rest of the conversation is in English. German would become the complete opposite, and we might use particular German phrases in other parts of our life when we are wanting to explain something we associate with the world of business-like negotiation. Or we might simply find ourselves rigidly sticking to one language despite the context calling for another to indicate our stance in relation to the people we are with, or the situation we are in. In this case it is the choice to switch or not that is symbolically significant.

> The linguist Hanan Ben Nafa studied the conversations between a group of her friends who were all Arabic and English bilinguals.[35] In fact, bilingualism was so natural to them that they all reflected on how challenging it can sometimes be to maintain a conversation with a monolingual Arabic or English speaker and stick to just one language. She found that while they *could* use either language to discuss almost everything they wanted to talk about, they tended to switch between languages quite systematically when talking about particular topics or when expressing certain attitudes. For example, she found that her friends would often switch from Arabic to English when giving compliments or expressing emotions. When prompted to reflect on when and why they switch in this way, one in the group explained that she knows how to express her feelings better in English.

Native naivety

I have one last point to make relating to the use of different languages, and it concerns some terminology that is often used when discussing who speaks what. It's very common to divide people into 'native' and 'non-native' speakers of a language. But what does this actually mean? And if we manage to work out what it means, why is it relevant? It's one of those concepts that might seem utterly obvious at a superficial level (depending on your own personal context), but as soon as you start looking a bit more closely it gets quite complex quite quickly.

For example, a native French speaker might have grown up in any one of a number of different countries, including places such as Cameroon, Senegal, Luxembourg, or France. Similarly, a native speaker of English might have grown up in Jamaica, South Africa, Sierra Leone, New Zealand, or many other countries all over the world. Yet the French of someone who grew up in Paris will sound quite different from the French of someone who grew up in Yaoundé. And the English of someone who grew up in Cape Town will sound quite different from the English of someone who grew up in Wellington. This is absolutely fine in most scenarios, but occasionally it becomes an issue. Because when do we hear the term 'native speaker'? Often, it's in the context of education, and especially language learning. You'll see adverts for language tuition, be that a language school, a university, or an individual, proudly boasting of their own or their staff's 'native speaker' status. And that makes sense, right? Of course we want to be taught by a native speaker, because they know the language best, and their use of it will be 'authentic'. This is all well and good until Mr and Mrs Jones, who are due to retire to their *gite* in Normandy next year and so are having private French lessons, come face to face with their new teacher, a native French speaker from Djibouti, and start to get a bit twitchy. Meanwhile, M and Mme Durand have recently moved to London and are paying top-rate fees for private English classes for their son, only to find out their teacher is a native English speaker from Singapore. Now, there is no reason why either teacher's abilities should be drawn into question. However, for Mr and Mrs Jones, M and Mme Durand, and many other language students around the world, these are unfortunately *not quite the right sort* of native speakers. Because not all native speakers are equal. Just as I suggested earlier that when Boris Johnson announced that everyone coming to Britain should learn to speak English he had a particular type of English in mind, when people use the term 'native speaker', especially in the context of language education, they have a particular version of the English language in mind. And who is accepted as a native speaker is heavily tied to issues of race, ethnicity, and nationality.

Before I became an academic linguist, I used to work as an English language teacher. My first job was abroad in a country I won't name only because I'm about to say something bad about the language school I worked at even though to be honest, this could have happened almost anywhere. Anyway, this language school, along with thousands like it throughout the world at the time (and also now, but less so) only employed native English speakers as teachers. At first, I'm ashamed to say, I didn't think much of it.[36] But after I'd been there a while and found myself peripherally involved in the recruitment process of new teachers, I did start to question it. I remember asking why they asked for a photograph as well as a CV from applicants (this is not usual at all for jobs in the UK as far as I know), and I was told that the owners of the language school were not keen on hiring teachers who they felt 'didn't look like native speakers', as the students might not accept them as such. And it turned out that determining whether someone would or would not be accepted as a native speaker had a lot more to do with the colour of their skin and their name, than it had to do with their knowledge of English. I'd like to say this was a one-off from the 1990s, and that things are better now. But it isn't, and they aren't. Among several academics working to explore and challenge the inequality on this area, Vijay Ramjattan is someone who clearly demonstrates through his work that 'non-white teachers, even when they identify as native English speakers, are deemed illegitimate speakers and teachers of the language',[37] and he sees English language teaching as 'aesthetic labour', because 'workers are expected to look and sound a particular way',[38] a way only white teachers can achieve with ease. We have a long way to go.

When things work differently

Throughout this book I've been describing speech as if we all experience it in similar ways. We acquire spoken language when we are young (perhaps monolingually, perhaps multilingually). The accent of that spoken language is determined to an extent by our surroundings, and then we adjust the way we speak, both consciously and unconsciously, as a way of negotiating our various identities within the different contexts we face. But not everybody has the same level of control over the way they speak. Some people face challenges in the processes of spoken language that give the whole subject of style-shifting a very different complexion. For example, people who stammer often have a quite different relationship with their spoken language when it comes to the role it plays in making them who they are. For many people who stammer, it is the stammer itself that does most of the identity work when it comes to their spoken language. The existence of the stammer defines them as a stammerer above everything else, with all other speech-related variation such as accent, or the use of particular speech features, playing a more secondary role. If our identities are created within our interactions with other people, then any interference with the natural process of interaction is bound to have an effect both on how we are perceived by others, and how we perceive ourselves.

Clare Butler, an academic who researches stammering and its effects in the workplace, talks of a process of 'identity cloaking' among her research participants, referring to a kind of veil that people place between themselves and society which gives them the space to deal with their stammer in their own way.[39] She found that for some people, especially those whose speech tended to be more fluent when they were in the role of 'expert' or 'team leader', the cloak divided their performance identity from their self identity. Because while for some people who stammer, the idea of having to perform might make their stammer worse, for others, the performance aspect is what helps with fluency. There are many examples of people's stammers disappearing when they sing,[40] and even, interestingly, when they consciously adopt a different accent.[41] Unsurprisingly, the advice from speech and language therapists for people who have this experience is not for them to then adopt another accent full time, for two reasons. Firstly, at some point, the 'new' accent could, in time, become your default speaking voice, causing the stammer to return. Secondly, putting on an accent in this way is, arguably, fundamentally changing who you are.

Incidentally, I have a stammer. It was worse when I was younger, and is only very slight now, but it is still there. Since being a teenager, I have gradually worked out in which situations it is most likely to appear, to the extent that I am now completely prepared for it, and it almost never takes me by surprise. I remember when I was at university it would appear when I had to speak in public in more formal situations, such as a class presentation. Thirty years later, I can still remember every detail of a presentation I had to give with my friend Mat, when I struggled with almost every line (or that's how it felt to me). Funnily enough, this was also the presentation in which I pronounced *Yosemite* (as in Yosemite National Park) as 'YOSamight', so it's not easy to forget! Even more notable was when I joined the drama society at university. I'd been involved in drama for years, and my friends at home knew the situation — if I had to read aloud from a script I would stammer, but if I'd learned the lines or had to improvise, I wouldn't. And I never stammered in a performance. But my new friends and other people at university didn't know this. In my first year I auditioned for a role in a bizarre retelling of Dracula. The audition simply involved performing something to 3 or 4 people, so I chose a scene from a play I'd been in at home. No problem. As a result, I was given the lead role of Dracula. But then at the next rehearsal the entire cast was together to read through the script we had just been given. I was introduced as the new boy, and off we went. This was almost my worse conceivable situation at the time — a room full of people I didn't know, and me reading out loud something I hadn't seen before. Obviously, I stammered, and obviously there was a lot of nervous shuffling and exchanged glances between people thinking, 'Who IS this guy?' and, 'What have we got ourselves into?'

These days, if you met me, you wouldn't know I had a stammer. Unless we were in a situation where I had to repeat myself due to background noise, or I had to say my name to someone I didn't know, especially on the phone. If I have to repeat my name to someone on the phone when there's background noise, I honestly might as well just give up! There is no question that, throughout my life, my stammer has had an effect on how people see me or how I see myself. I have no doubt that at certain times people will have seen me as quiet, or even rude, for not joining in a conversation, when in reality I have simply known that I would have struggled to say what I wanted to say. At other times people just think I'm odd for taking a big pause and a kind of gulp before saying my name, or else insisting on spelling it (a well-known technique for stammerers) when it really doesn't need spelling. I have visions of the person on the other end of a phone line suddenly paying attention, pen in hand, when I say I'll spell my name: 'D-R-U-M-M …' only for me to get to the end and them think, 'Hmm, I probably could have guessed that if I'm honest.'

But my stammer is very mild now. For people with stronger stammers or other speech impediments the challenges can be a lot more significant, potentially affecting our own and others' sense of who they are. It's not uncommon for people to be treated as though their speech impediment relates to some other kind of learning difficulty, resulting in people speaking past them to the person they are with, as if this other person is their carer.[42] Or else they will simply be hung up on when the person on the other end of the phone can't wait for them to finish their order to make their hair appointment.[43] How could this not affect someone's identity? In a fascinating podcast series by William Laven called *Stammer Stories*, which explores the experience of stammering from lots of different perspectives, people share their experiences of how their stammer has impacted their sense of who they are. Not only do people reflect on being reluctant to speak to people for fear of how they will be perceived, but also one guest spoke of how, because of this, when growing up, she wasn't used to actually hearing her own voice. Given the extent to which we use spoken language to create our identities, this is a fascinating insight.[44]

For these and other people there is very little choice at all in how they speak, or the extent to which they are able to do so. People affected by a stroke or a head injury may suddenly find that they have very little control over the muscles that help produce speech, rendering many of the details around accents we've been looking at throughout this book insignificant. And this lack of control will have an impact on the role their spoken language previously played in their sense of identity. Barbara Shadden, a professor in communication disorders, has described speech aphasia (problems with speech after damage to the brain) as 'identity theft', emphasising the serious effect it can have both on how we see ourselves and how others see us.[45] For some, there might be a complete lack of speech. It's not uncommon for people with cerebral palsy, for example, not to have the ability to speak at all. Some people in this situation have access to electronic speech aids that are controlled through eye tracking technology which leads to the output of synthesised speech. Up until recently, the speech it produced tended to be quite generic and robotic, but these days there are far more options. In 2021, a story circulated widely about a man called Richie Cottingham, from Hull in Yorkshire. Richie has cerebral palsy and relies on a speech aid to communicate, but he was frustrated with the voice it produced, as it was exactly the same voice as everyone else who uses a similar device. He wanted to sound different from other people, and yet similar to his friends and family, so his speech therapist, Jennifer Benson, helped him launch an appeal to find a new voice, a voice that better represented his identity as a man from Yorkshire. People were invited to donate their voices, at which point Richie narrowed them down to his favourites and the final three were blended together to create his new voice. Jennifer Benson said that it 'was critical to get the perfect voice for Richie — this voice will now express his identity and personality so it had to be just right, in the same way that we all have a voice that represents who we are and where we come from'.[46]

There's one more condition I'd like to mention that affects the way we speak, and which is especially relevant when exploring the link between our accents and our identities, even if it is very rare. In 2014, a woman named Julia Matthias was in the news in the UK due to the fact that a series of severe migraines had left her speaking with a foreign accent. Instead of her usual Essex accent, Mrs Matthias found herself speaking in a way that people variously perceived as South African, French, or Italian. She became one of only a few people in the UK with what's known as foreign accent syndrome. Given what we know about the link between our speech and identity, it is not surprising that Mrs Matthias has commented that the condition 'takes away your whole identity — you lose what was you'.[47] Instead of being viewed as a local in her hometown, she is asked, every day, where she comes from, purely on the basis of her speech.

Foreign accent syndrome is believed to be caused by damage to the speech production areas of the brain, often as a result of a stroke, head trauma, or migraines. The result is not a foreign accent as such, but rather alterations to specific speech sounds, which, when combined, give the impression of foreign-accented speech. The issue of course, is that the individual — often suddenly — has no, or very limited, control over those speech sounds, and, therefore, no control over the ways in which they are now perceived. The accent that they are perceived as having might be one that comes with a whole host of attitudes and prejudices within the particular society in which they live. So not only will they feel as though they have become someone else, and be treated as such, but also they might now be treated negatively by those who don't know them on the basis of negative stereotypes associated with their new perceived accent. Speech scientist Nick Miller has worked in this area, and he describes several examples of people with foreign accent syndrome desperately trying to come to terms with their new identity, be that through moving to a place where they felt their new accent would fit in, or even by changing their name.[48]

The fact is, nobody has complete and consistent control over all the various aspects of their speaking voice. Some aspects are easier to manipulate than others, and different people have different restrictions with regard to what they can and can't adjust. But most importantly, people have different views on what they might want to adjust, whether they can or not. Because it's these adjustments, or lack of adjustments, that help make us who we are. It's also these adjustments that help keep language alive and evolving. And that's a good thing.

CHAPTER 5

Soon we'll just be grunting to one another

Imagine if English ceased to be used in everyday life. Admittedly, there would have to be some kind of cataclysmic event, as the language is so embedded globally in terms of technology and media, but just imagine. Let's not get too dark by thinking about death and destruction, and pretend it could happen in a way that didn't include lots of people disappearing. Maybe we all suffered some kind of sudden linguistic memory loss but very quickly managed to replace everything we used English for with another language. From that point on English would stay as it was, with no people to use it and adapt it for their needs. It might go on to be learned as an academic exercise in order for people to understand some of the old texts and recordings that were still around, and to help historians understand life before The Great Language Purge, but it would no longer develop. Much like Latin today, which is still studied, and still valuable, but has no users who have learned it as a first language or who speak it as their primary language.

But this hasn't happened. There is a continual supply of new English speakers, and the language continues to change to suit the needs of those speakers. Back in Chapter 1 we looked at some of the changes that have occurred in English over the years. Taking a very broad view, we can confidently say that the English language has changed a lot since the days of Shakespeare, and we can even identify clear differences if we listen to recordings of people made only 50 years ago. But when and how do all these changes take place? Does language just naturally change, regardless of who's around, and we just hang on for the ride, using whatever version is in use at the time and adjusting the way we speak to keep up with the changes? Well, no, not really. People are the drivers of language change — we are what makes it happen. And advances in technology that enable communication to happen more rapidly and more widely help to speed up this process. If there weren't a continual supply of new speakers of English, acquiring it either as a first language or as a language learned later, who need to communicate with each other, then the process of change would grind to a halt.

Does this mean we all contribute to the process of change throughout our lives? Does our use of English gradually change as we move from childhood to adulthood, to middle age, to old age? Well, yes and no. But mainly no. Of course the way we speak changes through childhood and adolescence, and it might be that we acquire some of the subtle changes that are happening in our accent as we interact with other people, but when we reach adulthood our way of speaking tends to remain fairly stable. Yes, we will adopt new vocabulary as times change and we need new words to describe new things (especially in terms of new technology), as the common term for something that already exists changes (for example a wireless becoming a radio), or as we learn to use more inclusive language when talking about people. And yes, the quality of our voice will alter as we age. But unless we happen to be strongly affected by moving to a different area with a different accent, with such an effect being less likely once we reach adulthood anyway, things will generally stay more or less the same. Of course we all style-shift, so perhaps we should say that it's our repertoire of styles that will generally stay the same throughout adulthood, even if we might find ourselves using some styles more than others in different times throughout our lives.

Quintessential Queen

Now, you might be sitting there, in your 60s, reading this and thinking, 'Well, I speak completely differently from how I spoke in my 30s,' and you might well be right. But I would suggest that there has likely been a specific reason for this, such as a change of location, a job where you felt you needed to adopt a new way of speaking, a particularly strong influence from people around you who are important to you, and so on. Or else the changes you're hearing are perhaps less significant than you think. Also, it's actually quite hard to know for sure if your or anyone else's accent has changed over the years, as we are generally quite bad at objectively describing our own speech. In order to check, we would need a recording from a long time ago to act as a comparison. This might not be too difficult in itself, but then we need to consider the contexts in which the recordings were made. You might hear a recording of yourself giving a speech aged 25 in the 1990s, only to think it sounds nothing like you now, aged 50. But you'd have to replicate the context of giving the same kind of a speech, and your feelings of doing so aged 25 in order for it to be a fair comparison. Fifty-year-old you might be a far more confident public-speaker than 25-year-old you, and your style of speech might well show this. What we need is a recording of a situation where the speaking context is as close as it can be to what it was in the past. Even better would be a series of recordings of the same speaker in the same situation over a period of years.

Enter Queen Elizabeth II. The Queen delivered her Christmas Message on radio, then television, then also online every year but one, since 1952. In it, she reflected on the major events of the year just gone and her hopes for the year to come. The message was pre-recorded (it was delivered live prior to 1959), and so represents a fairly consistent, albeit rather formal, context for speech. It also provides an excellent source of linguistic data. The phonetician Jonathan Harrington and his colleagues took advantage of the consistency of the format of the Christmas Message across the years as a way of exploring whether someone's accent remains stable throughout their lives. They analysed and compared speeches from the 1950s with speeches from the 1980s to see if there were any changes in the Queen's pronunciation, especially of vowels (which, as we know, do a lot of the work when we're thinking about accents). They found that her vowel sounds had indeed changed slightly — they had drifted towards a more modern version of RP, or what Harrington and his colleagues call 'standard southern British English', an accent 'that is characteristic of speakers who are younger and/or lower in the social hierarchy'.[1] For example, the vowel sound in a word like *hat* changed from something like 'het' to something closer to how most people say it now. This part of their research is summarised in the aptly titled and very accessible 'Does the Queen speak the Queen's English?'[2] Obviously this is a very small sample (one),[3] and the Queen existed in a very unusual context, so we shouldn't read too much into it, but it is interesting. Her accent definitely changed. Well, the accent she used in this particular annual ritual changed, so perhaps it says more about the changing formality of the event itself than it does about any actual change in accent.

It's the youngers

So, if people's accents don't really change over the course of their lives without some kind of external influence, how does language itself keep evolving? Well, most of the magic happens between generations, and especially around the wonderfully innovative period of childhood and adolescence. Young people are generally seen to be at the forefront of language change, just as they are at the forefront of all sorts of societal changes in terms of behaviour, attitudes, and fashion. Young people are at a time in their lives when they are naturally working out who they are and where they fit in the worlds in which they find themselves. Many are simultaneously trying to separate themselves from their parents and the adults around them and trying to show solidarity with their own particular social groups. They are perhaps the most likely age group to experiment with how they look and behave in order to position themselves in relation to other people. And of course, part of this experimentation comes in the form of language, with young people using it as a resource as they assemble their particular identities. This has been happening for as long as people have been observing how language behaves, and we can assume it has been happening in similar ways throughout history. It might not have been the case that forging one's own identity has always played the central role for adolescents that it has done in more recent generations, certainly not in the sense of a defined and observable 'teenagerhood', but it would almost certainly have been the case that younger people were naturally quicker to adopt new ways of doing things and new ways of talking about things. It would perhaps not have been as conscious as it often is now, but it still happened. This less-conscious version of change would come in the form of small adjustments in pronunciations that come about through contact with different people as an individual aligns themselves with particular social groups, or the ready adoption of innovative words and phrases that they encounter. Modern-day teenagers actively distance themselves from people older (and younger) than them and use particular ways of speaking as one way of creating and maintaining that divide.

What helps to make adolescence an especially rich stage of life in terms of change is that pretty much the same thing is happening to a whole social group of people that are the same age. This doesn't generally happen in other areas of life. If you move to a new part of the country, at any age, it is just you and maybe other members of your family who are experiencing that same change of environment and societal expectations. If you migrate to another country, even if you do so alongside lots of other people who are doing the same thing, you are one among many people of different ages and with different goals. But when you move into and through adolescence, you are doing it alongside every single one of your peers. The linguist Gretchen McCulloch makes the point that we are especially likely to pick up new words and bits of language when we first enter a community.[4] And reaching adolescence is entering a community on a large scale. Just think of the linguistic innovation this sets in motion.

The linguistic creativity of adolescents, and their role in driving language change means that they are an especially carefully studied group when it comes to their language use. For example, linguist Penelope Eckert spent two years in the early 1980s researching youth speech in various high schools in Detroit. She spent a lot of time simply 'being' in one school in particular, observing how people interacted, listening to how they spoke, and gradually becoming part of school life. She was interested in observing the social practices of the students, not simply interviewing them and comparing the recordings solely based on broad demographic categories. During this process she noticed a clear opposition between two groups of students in particular — the largely pro-school, middle-class students referred to as the Jocks, and the broadly anti-school, working-class students referred to as the Burnouts. These groups represented the two extremes of the school population, with most students being part of the 'in-betweens', who would either be vaguely associated with one group or the other, or else desperate to avoid classification along these lines altogether. The two core groups engaged in different activities, wore different clothes, had different outlooks on life, and, crucially, used language in different ways. Eckert looked at all of these factors together to gain a picture of how they are all related. When you start looking at things in this way you unearth some intriguing relationships between certain practices. Who knew, for example, that the use of certain pronunciations could correlate with the width of the leg of a speaker's jeans? [5]

Another linguist and anthropologist, Norma Mendoza-Denton, spent several years in the 1990s carrying out similar ethnographic research in a Californian High School and its surrounding Latina community. Her primary focus was on the female members of two dominant gangs — the Norteña and the Sureña, who allied themselves with different values, social practices, and, again, used language in subtly different ways to each other, and to their peers from other backgrounds. For me, reading Mendoza-Denton's account of the research, called *Homegirls: language and cultural practice among Latina youth gangs*,[6] was what made things start to click into place regarding the use of specific speech features in the process of creating identities. She showed how simply pronouncing something a certain way, when combined with a specific use of eyeliner and a distinct way of walking, helps to successfully create an identity within a particular context.

Speaking like they do online

I mentioned earlier how the influence of television on the speech of young people is limited and temporary — that an American child picking up a few Britishisms from watching *Peppa Pig* during the Covid pandemic is unlikely to result in a permanent change.[7] However, there is no doubt that popular culture as a whole has some kind of influence on the way many young people speak. Much of this can be put down to the sheer ease with which TV, music, and videos can be shared, chopped up, repurposed, and re-shared these days compared to just a few years ago. Clips can be watched and re-watched with minimal effort, increasing people's exposure to the same innovative bits of language to an extraordinary degree. Catchphrases or lines from TV shows are no longer only revisited in the playground, they are made into memes and given whole new leases of life. And this inventiveness then filters into spoken communication, with savvy teens dropping phrases and pronunciations into their speech, leaving surrounding adults bewildered.

But some influences on the speech of young people seem to be a bit more permanent, or at the very least, slightly less fleeting. I've already mentioned Multicultural London English (MLE) a couple of times — that relatively recent linguistic development from London that has emerged largely as a result of contact between different languages and language varieties, but which has strong roots in Black varieties of British English. I've also mentioned Multicultural British English (MBE) — MLE combined with local accent features to create different versions in different urban centres of the UK. MLE and MBE are used by young people in lots of places in the UK, and they are a way of speaking that is increasingly common in various sections of popular culture. For a good representation of MLE you could explore the Netflix series *Top Boy,* where the naturally authentic language helps to bring Dushane, Sully, Dris, and all the other characters to life (and where I came across the term 'youngers', used in the heading for the previous section). For a good representation of MBE, you could seek out videos made by grime artists from around the UK. For readers who are not au fait with some of the more recent developments in popular music, grime is a British form of rap music — loud and energetic with usually fast, sophisticated lyrics, albeit with quite a bit of effing and jeffing.[8] Grime began in London (incidentally, Kano, one of the early pioneers of grime, is the actor who plays Sully in *Top Boy*), but spread throughout the country, and now it's also possible to find thriving grime scenes in places such as Manchester, Leeds, Liverpool, Birmingham, and Glasgow.

Just as the language and accent of traditional Country and Western music is Southern US, the accent of a lot of rock and pop music is some kind of vague generic mid-Atlantic, and the language of US rap is African American English, grime also has a default language: MLE. But unlike the vocals on most other types of music, UK grime especially allows for, and encourages, regional variation. So, while Kano, Dizzee Rascal, and Stormzy are most definitely from London, Bugzy Malone and Aitch are clearly from Manchester, Lady Leshurr is from Birmingham, and Hazey is definitely from Liverpool.[9] They are all using recognisable linguistic features of MLE, but they are also using other linguistic features that are more specific to their own local area. In other words, Multicultural British English. Perhaps it is this regional flexibility that has helped MBE spread into the speech of groups of young people across the UK. It isn't the case that they are indiscriminately imitating the London speech of the people they listen to on their phones — instead they are taking that way of speaking and making it their own.

Let's look at some specific examples from grime to illustrate what I mean. I'm unashamedly using some older (in music terms) examples, but then I am unashamedly older (in age terms) than most people who listen to grime.

In 'Spitfire' by Bugzy Malone you can hear features associated with MLE alongside features from Manchester.[10] MLE features include pronouncing *this* as 'dis' and *thing* as 'ting' ('th'-stopping), using a flattened vowel in words such as *out* and *about*, and a more emphasised 'oo' sound in words such as *student* and *two* (think of it as being close to the French word *tu*). Manchester features include using the northern England pronunciation of the vowel in *trust* and *up* (so that it's close to the vowel in *foot*) and the typically Manchester pronunciation of *spitfire* as something closer to 'spitfioh', with that last vowel being more like the 'o' sound in *got*.

And in 'Queen's Speech 4' by Lady Leshurr, you can hear MLE combined with a Birmingham accent.[11] She also has 'th'-stopping, and she uses 'gyal' instead of *girl*, which is a feature of MLE originating from Jamaican Creole. But the vowel in *dance* and *fast* is a Midlands one rather than a London one (rhyming with *trap*), and the first vowel sound in words such as *over* and *loaded* are distinctly Birmingham.

UK and US rap music has played an important role in the development of language for some young people over recent years, and it has influenced people's speech in ways that simply weren't possible in previous generations. This is down to two main reasons. The first reason isn't anything new; it is simply that a lot of rap, both in the UK and US represents a lifestyle and an attitude that is intrinsically attractive to a lot of young people. It is cool, edgy, and tough, and so its proponents are imitated by others in order to capture some of that coolness for themselves. But the same is true for many music styles over the years. The second reason is that music such as grime and drill (and its US counterparts) is immersive, at least for some people. It isn't music that is passively listened to, it is music that is inhabited and created by the people engaging with it.

Back in 2014, I was doing some research with young people aged 14–16 who had been permanently excluded from mainstream school and were being educated in what is known as a Pupil Referral Unit. Most of the boys were into rap or grime to varying degrees. But what was interesting was the extent to which rapping slipped into their everyday communication, often mid-conversation. In-jokes and insults were shouted across the room or muttered under their breath in the unmistakeable style of rap. And it wasn't uncommon at breaktime to find a group of boys huddled in a group trying out their newly crafted lines over a tinny beat from a phone. This will come as no surprise if you've ever watched a grime or drill video. Ninety per cent of them involve a group of young men moving and hanging around someone who has taken centre stage against an inner-city backdrop, rapping over a pulsing backing track. And for every more polished video you come across, there are hundreds more that are shared between friends or uploaded to some online platform or another. This is why UK rap has had such an effect on the language of so many groups of young people — it isn't just something you listen to, it's something you do, and it can even be something you live. The language is part and parcel of being that person. As the well-known British rapper Dave says: grime is 'like a sound, culture, style — the way that [you] dress and speak'.[12]

Language is going to the dogs

Much of my own research aims to challenge the negative perceptions that often surround the language of young people, especially in relation to Multicultural London English, or Multicultural British English. Sometimes also known by the pejorative label 'Jafaican', this way of speaking is frequently the target of scorn and ridicule in the British mainstream media and elsewhere, despite it being a perfectly natural language development in urban centres in the UK and, in other forms, Europe. We've seen how speaking in ways that don't match the expected 'standard' variety can cause problems for people, and young people are in a situation where they are especially vulnerable to such judgements, as they often are the innovators of linguistic diversity. Negative perceptions and misinformation around youth language can be potentially extremely damaging, and young people can be misunderstood or deliberately misinterpreted or misrepresented because their way of speaking does not conform to the expected 'standard' variety.

All of this linguistic innovation doesn't go unnoticed by the adults that come into contact with these young people, whether that be family and teachers, or older people tutting as they walk past a group of them at the bus stop or in the shopping centre. It is at the point of adolescence that the differences in language use between the generations becomes especially apparent, and the days of the adults in their lives routinely shaping the way young people speak are pretty much over. The disapproval of the older generations regarding the younger generations' use of language has become a bit of a cliché, but it's a cliché that continues to be based in fact. It's tempting to think that this is a recent thing, with online articles claiming that young people are 'literally talking themselves into unemployment' demonstrating how bad the situation has become these days, but it's a pattern that has been repeated throughout history, with each generation lamenting the linguistic inadequacies of those people one or two generations below.[13] Once again it comes down to most people simply not liking the fact that language changes, and so when they see those changes (or differences that they fear will become long-term changes) happening right in front of them, they push back. The lexicographer Peter Sokolowski makes the astute observation that 'most English speakers accept the fact that the language changes over time, but don't accept the changes made in their own time'.[14] In other words, everyone knows that we don't use English like Shakespeare did, and that's absolutely fine, but their understanding runs out when it comes to their daughter 'saying "like" every other word'. People often have fairly inflexible ideas as to how English should be used, and those ideas tend to correspond with what they were taught at school, and the way English was used at the time they personally reached adulthood and their own language became fairly fixed. When you learn that a particular grammatical structure or pronunciation is 'correct' and that others are 'incorrect', it's very hard to let go of that.

In a TED talk from 2013, the linguist John McWhorter gives examples of adults complaining about the language of young people from various points in the past, all of which sound very similar to comments made today.[15] He shows the views of a college professor in 1956, and then a schoolteacher in 1917, who claims that 'every high school is in despair because its pupils are so ignorant of the merest rudiments [of spelling and punctuation]'. Similar views were expressed by the President of Harvard in 1871, and a county superintendent of schools in 1841. Finally, McWhorter provides an example from 63 AD, in which a 'pedant' writes: 'Spoken Latin has picked up a passel of words considered too casual for written Latin, and the grammar people use when speaking has broken down. The masses barely use anything but the nominative and the accusative ... it's got to the point that the student of Latin is writing in what is to them an artificial language, and it is an effort for him to recite in it decently[!]' Although these examples focus primarily on writing rather than speaking, historical criticisms exist across both uses of language, if only because people often find it hard to separate the two.

If you are a parent, grandparent, or carer you no doubt have your own examples of things that young people say that you can't help reacting to, whether that takes the form of a comment and 'correction', or simply an inward seethe or shudder. And when you think back to your own teenage years and remember that something similar also happened to you, you probably dismiss the relevance of that comparison because the young people you are dealing with use language that is a lot worse, more annoying, or more likely to interfere with their job prospects than you not pronouncing your 't's every now and then or saying something was 'cool'. Or else you might think that what you are doing is very much the same as what happened to you, and quite right too; it might have been a bit annoying when someone corrected the way you spoke, but now you can see that it was the right thing to do, and it helped you become the person you are! Either way, it's a cycle that will always continue, even if the young people now vow that they would never do anything like this to their future children. When I talk to teenagers about this I always ask if their parents, carers, or teachers ever comment negatively on the particular things they say, and there is always a murmur of recognition followed by a few predictable examples such as saying 'like' too much, using slang, or using 'lazy pronunciations'. But then I tell them that they will very likely be having similar conversations with their own or other children when they are older — unless, of course, they decide to study sociolinguistics in which case they'll be too interested in the language features themselves to worry about policing their use.[16] A few times a year I get the pleasure of introducing the topic to mixed groups of parents and teenagers when they attend the university open day and I'm asked to talk a bit about what sociolinguistics is. When I mention adults getting frustrated by the overuse of 'like', or rising intonation, or the use of TikTok slang, I get some understanding looks from the adults. When I then go on to explain why criticism along these lines is problematic, arbitrary, and unfair, the mood shifts and, as one, all the young heads swivel accusingly towards nervously laughing parents. And we could take this further. I'm not accusing any individual parents on those university open days of discriminating against their own children, but isn't it all part of a familiar pattern where older people are dismissive and critical of younger people's lives? Not only do they not use English properly, but they don't know the meaning of hard work, and it's their own fault they can't afford a mortgage because they spend all their money on avocado on toast and Netflix.[17]

What often triggers misunderstanding around the language of young people is the inability to separate spoken language from written language. This lack of separation can be an issue at school, a place that many people feel should be strict on promoting 'standard' English, even if they don't necessarily understand what that might look like. Now, I'm not a schoolteacher, but I do spend a lot of time talking to schoolteachers (mainly, admittedly, teachers of English), and I generally try to stay clued-up about discussions around language in schools, particularly in the UK. Like any profession, teachers can have very different views from one another, and can approach similar things in different and contradictory ways depending on their own experience, viewpoints, and beliefs. Unless a teacher has had specific training or education in some of the areas of sociolinguistics that we have been looking at in this book, then it's easy to see how they might feel that the implementation of policies that insist on pupils 'speaking in standard English in the classroom', and 'answering in complete sentences' is the most sensible approach.[18]

But what does it mean to speak in standard English in the classroom? How standard is standard enough? Should they be speaking as if reading from a script? And what makes a sentence complete? Must it have a certain number of words? Must it repeat the question as part of the answer in order for there to be no doubt that this is indeed the question that is being answered? If you start to question the details of these kinds of approaches in this way, things soon start to unravel. Because language is, as we have already seen, messy. But even if a particular teacher was able to clarify precisely what they meant by the terminology, the most pertinent question then becomes, 'But, why?' The thing is, nobody naturally speaks in standard English, at least not consistently. As we have seen, people can use standard English features (or not), but the blanket term is better suited to describe certain forms of written English. And nobody speaks in complete sentences, at least in the sense implied by these sorts of policies. So why would we choose to encourage people to use language in a way that is simply unnatural? If your answer is that it helps children with their writing, then are you sure this is really the best way to do that? If so, then I think quite a few people would like to see your evidence.

Luckily, every school will have at least a few English teachers. And if we're really lucky, those English teachers will have had a bit of sociolinguistics education as part of their training and will have the knowledge to counter such policies with their linguistic insights.[19] However, the reality is often that the clued-up teacher isn't in a position to effectively challenge such practices (perhaps they are too junior, or their specialism is marginalised), and so the policy limps along in all its inadequacy. I've certainly spoken to teachers who know full well how meaningless and problematic such approaches can be, and yet who feel obliged to maintain the façade of trying to make all of their wonderfully linguistically diverse students speak in the same non-diverse way by following these kinds of arbitrary rules. They are fully aware that if certain groups of young people are routinely falling short of a set of prescribed standards in the use of language, then the problem is likely to be in the criteria against which we are assessing them rather than in the way they actually communicate.

Slanguage

But it's not just the fact that young people don't speak or use language 'properly' that bothers some members of older generations, it's also their use of what they see as slang. Never mind that older people had their own slang when they were younger — does 'groovy' and 'far out' ring any bells for anyone? What about 'wicked' and 'sound'? It's easy to dismiss slang as a less-serious form of language that comes in and out of fashion and which changes as someone moves from adolescence to adulthood as their communication needs and contexts change. But spoken language is about far more than simply a way of communicating messages between people. Yes, it has that function, but it does so much more than this. The way in which something is said can carry as much, if not more, meaning as the content of the message itself, and the very act of speaking serves so many more purposes than straightforward communication, both for the speaker and for the listener. We've looked at how this is the case in terms of accents and dialects associated with particular regions, social classes, genders, ethnicities and so on, but what about the words and phrases themselves? What's going on when we hear people using words like feds, pot, wicked, narc, epic, safe, lush, bare, shook or (less likely), bona, dolly, luppers, vada, and ajax? All of these would be seen as slang: colloquial, non-standard language that is often innovative, routinely looked down upon, and usually associated with particular groups of people.

Slang plays a really important role in relation to both personal, and social identity. Its use in a given context cannot fail to provide some kind of information about the speaker: be that group membership or allegiance, knowledge and experience about a particular way of life, or attitude and stance towards an aspect of society. By using slang appropriately we are saying 'I am an insider, I am part of this group' — or at the very least 'I want to be (seen as) part of this group' — and at the same time we are testing the insider/outsider status of others. Imagine a group of teenagers, and one uses the phrase 'I'm shook' (meaning I'm surprised or shocked) for the first time, having heard it online. Those in the know might agree with the sentiment, but what will those who haven't come across it do? Will they dare to reveal their outsider status by asking what it means?

By the same token, slang can be used to exclude people deliberately and explicitly, or at least leave them in a state of bewildered ignorance. Perhaps a good example of such slang is Polari — the almost forgotten secret language of gay men in England.[20] Certainly, words such as bona, dolly, and luppers would not mean much to most people these days, even gay men. But in the 1960s and 70s, when gay sex was still a crime (and lesbian sex simply didn't exist, apparently), it provided a way of secretly signalling a gay identity to other gay men. It was at the same time inclusive, and actively exclusive.

What's interesting about today's slang is that it changes so quickly and seems so impenetrable to outsiders. The speed of change can probably be put down, at least in part, to the sheer volume of communication that takes place between young people today. When I was a teenager in the 1980s, my contact with friends and people my own age was limited to three contexts. We'd see each other at school; we'd meet up and see each other out of school, maybe at something organised like a sport or music thing or some kind of gathering, but usually just aimlessly hanging out; or we'd speak on the phone (yes, actually speaking on an actual telephone that was attached to the wall). Teenagers in the 2000s would have been in a fairly similar situation, although they would have also been communicating online through things like MySpace and MSN Messenger, and they might have had phones where they could send text messages (albeit with a character limit and a charge per message). Compare that to how things are now. Some things remain the same. Adolescents still go to school, and many still hang out with friends in person. Speaking on the phone is simply not a thing anymore, certainly not between young people of the same age, but it has been replaced by countless additional methods of communication in the form of messaging not only through straightforward and limitless text/SMS/iMessage/WhatsApp, but also through apps such as TikTok, Snapchat, and Instagram. And this messaging happens at incredible speed with different people across different conversations simultaneously. Then you have some groups of people playing games online while simultaneously talking to other players through headsets and messaging each other on Discord. Just think of the vast amount of language that is involved in maintaining all that communication. And just think of all the ways in which that language might be adapted and adjusted along the way. We know that changes in language spread through people coming into contact with one another and shaping the language between them, and there are far more contexts for this to happen than there ever were before. Not only are people messaging each other and using language that way, they are also sharing, commenting on, and creating social media content themselves in the form of Snapchat and Instagram stories and TikTok videos. All of this requires an understanding of whatever language is appropriate to that context, and an ability to manipulate that language in new and creative ways, ways which often leave older generations confused. So much so in fact that helpful guides to teen slang appear almost weekly online.[21] But don't ever tell me that young people don't know how to communicate any more. Many of them are communicating in ways and at a rate that is almost unimaginable to older people. It's just a different form of communication.

And this shouldn't come as a surprise to anyone. As we've seen, language has always been used as a way of maintaining group boundaries, and the generation gap between adults and adolescents represents a fairly significant boundary. Just as parents of now-60-year-olds probably shook their heads in bewilderment at the 1970s-inspired slang that their offspring once produced, parents now shouldn't be surprised when they notice that they can't fully understand what their teenage children and their friends are saying; that's kind of the point. One group has their way of speaking and the other group has theirs.

> Every now and then I ask some young people to let me know what slang words and phrases they are using that older people might not understand. Here's a few from the 2020s, although they will already be out of date by the time you read this book. If you want to know what they all mean, ask an expert.*
>
> AF, extra, fire, flex, goals, lit, lowkey, mood, no cap, ONG, periodt, salty, shook, slay, stan, tea, wig, vibes.
>
> *A young person, that's the point.

Who makes this stuff up?

There are two ways of looking at the innovative use of language that has been developed, and is continuing to develop, within social media or online communication. Firstly, we can explore its use as a form of written language.[22] Secondly, we can explore the ways in which the language has moved from the screen into actual speech. But before we do either, we need to look at where this language actually originates. How do new words, expressions, and ways of saying things actually come to be used by young people on social media in the first place? Where do they come from?

Many of the words, phrases, and pronunciations that find their way into the language repertoire of social media savvy teens in the UK, US, and Australia originated in African American English (AAE), or a combination of AAE, the US drag scene, and LGBTQ+ communities. White people using language from AAE has been a thing for a long time. Gretchen McCulloch describes it as 'borrowing coolness from another group'.[23] A similar thing has been happening in the UK for decades, with the language of Black youth culture being seen as having its own prestige by many young people.[24] On a surface level you could perhaps look at this and see it simply as the continued process of language variation and change — people adopting the language features they come into contact with because they are drawn to them for whatever reason, and then bringing them into their own social groups, who then also start using them, and so on. But that really is on the surface. Dig a little deeper and it starts to look a lot more like the dominant groups culturally appropriating the language features with which marginalised social groups have tried to amplify their own voices.

The reason this can happen so freely, with the speakers who adopt these language features arguably unaware of what they are doing, is that the language, in their minds, is associated with social media rather than with the communities where it originated. To a middle-class white teenager from Manchester, or Phoenix, or Melbourne, peppering their social media posts and even conversations with words and phrases such as slay, shook, and hella might feel like they are simply adopting the latest social media linguistic trends. They probably don't think too much about it — they see something being used online by their friends, they figure out the context, and they start using it themselves. If asked about it, they would likely see it simply as a kind of slang (I know this because I have asked them). But it isn't just adopting a kind of slang, its more than that. It's taking words, phrases, and pronunciations from other cultures with no recognition of those cultures and of the history behind those bits of language. And when there is such a clear inequality between the cultures whose language is being appropriated, and the white mainstream culture doing the appropriation, then this is problematic.

If you're not convinced, then think back to the discussion in a previous chapter about when people using Black varieties of English need to style-shift or code-switch in certain situations, sometimes for their own safety. Think about how the Black people describing their experiences were negatively judged or even at risk of death for using language associated with Black culture. And then contrast that with the ways in which young white people can adopt the very same speech features and yet remain safe. There has been a lot written about this, but to pick one example, here is a quote from an article by Aarony Bailey:

> My issue with non-Black people using Black slang is that they will never receive any backlash for doing so. They can say 'bruv' (brother) and be labelled as cool, urban, and youthful. But when, as a Black woman I say 'bruv', I'm seen as ghetto, lower class, and unintelligent. This double standard is not the fault of the non-Black person using the language, but more so the fault of

those who choose to put Black people into a box, despite them behaving in exactly the same way that non-Black people do.[25]

It's very easy to find out the extent to which the language being used by young people online originated in AAE or Black British English, just look at one of the many resources online.[26] But what should be done about it? What can be done about it? Once a language feature has been embedded into social media language, it isn't going anywhere until it is replaced by the latest trend. However, what we can do is encourage people to become aware of the original context of the language they use in order to at least give them the full picture. In an excellent article on the subject, Imani Benberry suggests that 'non-Black people should remove themselves from communities online and in real life that pressure them to adopt the speech patterns of African Americans ... If you do end up using AAVE occasionally, then at the very least supporting Black lives and communities in loud and consistent ways should also be a part of your online engagement.'[27]

Write how you speak

It's our responsibility to learn more about the language we use. And this has never been truer than now, when all things linguistic are taking such a fascinating turn due to the online world. Not so long ago it was relatively easy, and often useful in various situations, to distinguish between written English and spoken English. The two were, or at least could be, very different things serving very different purposes. The English you need when writing a job application letter is not the same as the English you need when you've got the job and you are chatting to new colleagues in the canteen. Even relatively informal written English found in a personal letter or postcard (remember those?) is different from the English you would use if you were telling the same person the same information face to face. In spoken English, we often use sentences that would appear incomplete when written down, we might repeat ourselves, or use fillers such as 'erm', and 'you know', and 'like', and then of course we can rely on gesture and body language to help get our message across. Understanding that the two forms of language are different is an important piece of knowledge, especially when you are learning how to use English effectively, either at school or as an adult learning English.

But things aren't so simple anymore, as the distinction between writing and speech has been well and truly blurred, at least in some areas. Yes, the original distinctions still exist in that we need to write in a certain way in a formal letter and other more rigid contexts. And, even in the past, there were always a few exceptions to the clear boundaries, for example, where do quickly scribbled notes sit? Are they spoken language written down? Or what about formal speeches — written language said out loud? But online communication has really shaken things up. In many ways, the language we use in messages and on social media is indeed spoken language written down. But then in other ways it is so much more than this. It's probably better to see it as simply another form of language that sits alongside written and spoken. All three have their own rules and conventions, albeit each with a lot of internal variation and fuzzy, overlapping borders.

One especially interesting feature of online language is the way it can be used to suggest particular accent differences, especially in the spelling it uses. This is something that tends not to happen in other types of writing. Most writing, whether it's formal and therefore rigidly following standard grammar and punctuation rules and conventions, or less formal and therefore perhaps being a bit more flexible in grammar and punctuation, will nevertheless tend to use standard spelling. Because writing itself doesn't have an accent; an accent is a property of speech. There are of course exceptions to this — the most obvious being written dialogue in novels or other texts. But most writing is accent-free on the page, ready to be given an accent by whoever says it out loud.

However, online language is often given an accent by the writer. People on social media can write in ways that attempt to replicate or at least suggest a particular pronunciation. Perhaps they are trying to show their own accent and own way of speaking; perhaps they are trying to imitate someone else; perhaps they are using a stereotypical feature in order to mock someone or to make a joke. A group of linguists did some work on this a few of years ago by looking specifically at how certain features of northern English accents were represented through different spellings on Twitter.[28] By attempting to indicate their own accent in this way, people are using their social media posts in ways that are similar to how they use their speech in other situations — as a method of foregrounding and even performing their regional identities. Another brilliant example of this is 'Scottish Twitter'— an area of Twitter that almost has its own cult status in terms of its humour and use of language. Linguists E. Jamieson and Sadie Ryan describe its backstory in their online article from 2019,[29] including plenty of examples such as, 'I deh trust the dentist when they start talking in code about your teeth to their wee pal, you got suhin to say say it to ma face prick.'[30]

Looking at online language in this way actually tells us some quite interesting things about accents, or, more specifically, what people notice about accents. If somebody tries to replicate accent features in writing through respellings, it will be the most salient or noticeable features they try to respell. So by looking at what they choose to emphasise we can tell which bits of their own or other people's accents they feel make those accents stand out. This can be especially intriguing when it's your own accent that people are trying to imitate. I recently saw a collection of tweets where Americans were trying to imitate what 'British' people sound like.[31] For example: 'British people be like munday, chewsday, wensday, thuhsday, FROIday, sa-a-day, sunday'.[32] There's lots going on here, but look in particular at how 'thuhsday' indicates non-rhoticity (or not pronouncing the 'r') and 'sa-a-day' suggests the use of glottal stops instead of 't's. In fact, 't'-glottaling is one that seems to come up a lot, with people posting pictures of water bottles and saying that British people say this is a 'wah uh boh uhl'.

The fact that such tweets exist is a result not only of the technology being there to give people a platform from which to share their observations, but also of the technology being there to provide that exposure to other varieties of language in the first place. Twenty years ago, your average American's experience of British accents would be from whatever British TV programmes were being shown, plus that guy Steve at work who grew up in Bedford. Oh, and maybe Elton John combined with some imaginary version of how English aristocracy speak. Likewise in the UK, the average person's experience of US accents would be from TV and film, and their experience of Australian accents would be from *Neighbours* or *Home and Away* (or in the case of me and my friend Luke, *Prisoner Cell Block H*). But things are different now. TikTok, YouTube, and Instagram give us immediate and infinite access to ways of speaking we wouldn't come across any other way. Put simply, we are exposed to more language and more variety than ever before. And this can't not be having an effect on the way our own language develops.

So yes, English is changing, and it might be changing more rapidly than ever before. Young people are doing what young people are supposed to do — they are innovating, experimenting, and playing with language in ways that often confuse, exclude, and sometimes irritate older people. But it shouldn't just be young people. We are all allowed to experiment with language. We should all feel able to push the various social and linguistic boundaries that surround us, even if it's just a little bit. We should absolutely be more aware of the histories and backstories of some of the linguistic innovations we come across before we decide whether it's appropriate to add them to our own repertoires, but that shouldn't make us afraid to experiment in our own ways.

Postscript

So where does this leave us? Right at the beginning of the book I asked you to think about the way you speak, and the way people around you speak. Throughout, I have invited you to reflect on your own and other people's attitudes towards those ways of speaking, with the suggestion that such attitudes are always about more than just language. Have any of those reflections and attitudes changed now that we're at the end? If I've done a half-decent job with this book, then I'm hoping for one of three outcomes, depending on your awareness of the subject before you started reading.

If you were someone who didn't know much about language when you started, but were keen to find out more, then I hope I've managed to provide you with something valuable, interesting, and possibly thought-provoking. At the very least, I hope I've provided a few linguistic facts and encouraged you to notice a bit more about how you and those around you use language. If I've managed to reach the point where you actually remember one of the facts or examples in the book and subsequently attempt to relay it to a friend or family member over dinner (however accurate or otherwise your retelling of it may be), then I will be delighted. But equally, I'd be very happy for you to disagree with some of the things I've said. A lot of this is my opinion or my take on a subject. It's a subject that I know something about, but so too do a lot of other very clever people. In the words of the film critic Mark Kermode, other opinions are available. And those opinions are worth listening to. Talking about language is always good, and disagreements about language use can be useful. It's when we stop reflecting on, and accepting, the flexible and changing nature of language and its impact on our lives that things go wrong.

If you were someone who knew a lot of this anyway, be that through past or current language study, or simply through linguistic interest, then I simply hope that I have provided a few more examples and anecdotes to back up your understanding. If I've managed to fill in any gaps, or made you think about things in a slightly different way, then even better.

Finally, if you've come to this book reluctantly, perhaps as someone who isn't really interested in language but got given this as a present ('Great, thanks. You really shouldn't have. Really, really shouldn't.'), or perhaps as someone who feels quite strongly about the idea of 'speaking properly', then this is a bit trickier. If you're the former, and you've managed to stick with it, then I genuinely hope that you came across at least a few things that you found interesting. I mean I'm not expecting people to become language enthusiasts overnight as a result of reading this, but I do honestly think that if more people knew even a little bit about how language works, then our own various worlds would be better places. If you're the latter, and you came to this with an attitude of 'come on then, prove me wrong', then I guess all I can hope for is that you have at least reflected on where your opinions on linguistic correctness have come from, and whether they are actually sustainable. Or fair.

Whatever your views and interests, there is no escaping the fact that for anyone who is able to speak or hear, spoken language plays an important role in our day-to-day lives. I've claimed here that in many ways it helps make us who we are. I've also suggested that once we understand that this is the case, then we need to do a lot better at accepting linguistic diversity. The societal inequalities that exist and which are played out, in part, through language are real and serious. I'm not suggesting that we can challenge those inequalities simply by knowing a bit more about language. But I am suggesting that we need to understand the role of language in creating and maintaining those inequalities before we can even begin to address them.

It's a start simply acknowledging and being interested in the immense power of spoken language — not just what is said, but how it is said. When you accept its role in making us who we are and how we perceive other people, you start to notice all sorts of things about your own speech and the speech of others. And honestly, it becomes a bit of a superpower. It becomes almost impossible to be bored in any situation where people are talking, even if they aren't talking to you. You start to notice individual pronunciations that are different from yours, or phrases which you've never heard before. You think about how those different sounds are made, and how you feel about that bit of grammar. I mean, you have to be subtle in public, but technically, is it really still eavesdropping when you are focusing on how someone is talking rather than what they are talking about?

And there's nothing wrong with taking pride in your own way of speaking. Obviously not in a way that suggests yours is any better than anyone else's, but certainly in a way that makes it equal with others; and accepting its role in making you, you. But maybe don't explicitly ask people for opinions on the way you speak unless you are fully prepared for the answer. I remember the time a few years ago when I was giving a talk in a school near Newcastle in the north-east of England, home of some wonderful accents and dialects. As part of the session, I asked the students to think about their own accents, and then I asked them to describe mine. One boy put his hand up and simply said, 'Vanilla'. Ah well.

Glossary

Accent The way in which someone pronounces the sounds of spoken language. Unlike dialect, which relates also to words and grammar, accent refers only to pronunciation.

Accent features Specific sounds or pronunciations of sounds that relate to a particular accent.

African American English (AAE) A variety of language that is strongly associated with Black and African American people in the United States. Like any language, it is systematic, rule governed, and varies between different groups of people. It is sometimes also known as African American Vernacular English (AAVE) or African American Language (AAL).

Accent reduction The process of deliberately learning how to make an accent less noticeable. As it is objectively impossible to speak without an accent, it is really a process of replacing one accent with another, more socially desirable one.

Black British English (BBE) A variety of language that is associated with the Black British population. Strongly influenced by Jamaican language (also known as Jamaican Creole or Patois) and West African languages.

BBC Pronunciation/BBC English The prestigious accent that is most strongly associated with BBC news readers, especially in previous decades. Also known as Received Pronunciation.

Bilingual Speaking two languages fluently.

Bi-dialectical Being able to use two distinct dialects naturally.

Creaky voice/Vocal fry A way of speaking in which the voice drops to a very low pitch, resulting in a rough, creaking quality.

Code-switching Moving between different ways of speaking depending on the context. Code-switching is often used to refer specifically to moving between different languages but can also be used to describe moving between styles within the same language. The latter is also known as style-shifting.

Dialect A variety of language that is associated with a particular group of people or a particular geographic region. It includes words, grammar, and pronunciation (accent).

Ethnographic An approach to research where the researcher embeds themselves (to varying degrees) within the community, culture, or context they are investigating. Common in areas such as anthropology and sociology.

Foreign accent syndrome A rare condition, often the result of damage to the brain, that affects the production of speech. The altered speech sounds give the impression of 'foreign' accented speech.

Glottal stop The sound that is made by stopping and then releasing airflow through the glottis (vocal folds). In English, the glottal stop is often used as a replacement for the 't' sound in words such as *matter* or *butter*. This process is known as t-glottaling, but is commonly referred to as dropping your 't's.

G-dropping The common (if slightly inaccurate) name given to the process of pronouncing words ending with '-ing' such as walking and swimming, as 'walkin'' and 'swimmin''.

GLOSSARY

Habitual be A feature of African American English where 'they be chatting' means they often, or habitually chat, rather than that they are necessarily chatting right now.

Hypercorrection Overdoing an attempt to use a more prestigious feature of language and getting it 'wrong' as a result. For example, 'He gave it to Luca and I.'

Intonation/Intonation pattern The pitch pattern of spoken language.

Jargon Words or phrases that are used by a specific group of people in a specific context. Often work or hobby related.

Lexical variation Language variation at the level of words. For example, bap, barm, muffin, and cob are all different words for a bread roll in the UK.

Lexis The words of a language.

Linguistics The study of language.

Linguistic profiling Assuming a person's social characteristics (such as their class or race) based on their voice.

Multicultural British English (MBE) A variety of English used by people in the UK that incorporates features associated with Multicultural London English alongside features from their regional accent or dialect.

Multicultural London English (MLE) A variety of English found in London that has emerged through contact between different languages and language varieties, but which has its roots in Black varieties of British English.

Monophthong/Diphthong A monophthong is a vowel sound that has the same quality throughout its duration (e.g. the 'ee' in 'sheep'); whereas a diphthong is a vowel sound that moves between two sounds (e.g. the 'oy' in 'boy').

Monolingual Speaking only one language.

Matched guise technique A technique used in accent attitude research that attempts to isolate people's feelings towards an accent specifically, as opposed to voice quality more generally. It does this by including among the recordings to be assessed the same speaker using two different accents. Any difference between people's feelings towards these two recordings must therefore be down to accent alone, as all other aspects of the voice will be the same.

Native/Non-native speaker People who have a particular language as their mother tongue vs people who have acquired a particular language later in life. The terms can be very problematic; for example, in relation to language teaching, when native speakers are falsely assumed to have greater expertise than non-native speakers, and native speakers from some backgrounds are afforded a higher status than those from other backgrounds.

Overt prestige/Covert prestige An accent or dialect is seen as having overt prestige when it matches mainstream society's views on what a 'standard' or prestigious way of speaking sounds like. An accent or dialect is seen as having covert prestige when it is clearly 'non-standard' but has value within a particular social group.

Phonetics/phonology Phonetics is the study of the production and perception of speech sounds. Phonology is the study of the ways in which those sounds are organised into language.

Phonological variation Variation in spoken language at the level of sound. For example, the word matter in English can be pronounced either with a 't' sound, with a 'd' sound, or with a glottal stop, but the meaning is the same.

Prefix Part of a word that is added to the beginning of a word to change its meaning. For example: *un*kind, *re*appear, *ir*replaceable.

GLOSSARY

Polari A type of slang historically associated with gay men, but which was also used by other persecuted groups as a secret form of communication.

Received Pronunciation/Modern RP The accent of English that is represented in British dictionaries and which serves as a model for most English language teaching. It retains prestige through its historical association with the educated upper classes of England and with the BBC.

Rhoticity/Rhotic The pronunciation of the 'r' sound in all contexts. A rhotic accent (or a rhotic speaker) is an accent (or speaker) that has or displays rhoticity. A non-rhotic accent or speaker will not pronounce the 'r' in certain contexts; for example, in words such as far and horse.

Raciolinguistics The area of study that examines the relationship between language and race, and how they each influence our understanding of the other.

Sound system The organisation of speech sounds within a particular language or dialect.

Sociolinguistics The area of academic study that explores the relationship between language, people, and society.

Speech feature A part of spoken language that we can use to help describe a particular accent, dialect, or way of speaking. For example, a particular vowel sound, tone of voice, or pronunciation.

Style-shifting Moving between different styles of speaking, usually within the same language. For example, using more or less formal speech depending on the context.

Suffix Part of a word that is added to the end of a word to change its meaning or grammatical nature. For example: beauti*ful*, kind*ness*, employ*ment*.

Triglossic A triglossic situation is where three languages serve three different functions in a particular society. For example, one might be associated with government, one with religion and learning, and one with everyday interaction.

The Great Vowel Shift A period of significant change in the vowel system of English that is generally seen to have taken place between the 15th century and the 18th century, resulting in several vowels (and therefore words) being pronounced differently.

Translanguaging Translanguaging describes a way of thinking about how people use multiple languages. Rather than seeing languages as being distinct entities with clearly defined borders, it views the process of using multiple languages as drawing on all of the linguistic resources that are available depending on the context.

Uptalk/Australian Questioning Intonation/High-rising terminal
A feature of speech in which the pitch of the voice gets higher at the end of a sentence, so it can sound a bit like the speaker is asking a question, even when they aren't.

Voiced/Voiceless consonants Voiced consonants use the voice in their production (the vocal folds vibrate), whereas voiceless consonants do not use the voice (the vocal folds do not vibrate). The 'z' in zoo and the 'b' in bed are voiced; the 's' in see and the 'p' in pet are voiceless.

Notes

Preface

1. Helen Pidd, 'BBC's Steph McGovern says she would earn more if she was posher', *The Guardian* (2018), https://www.theguardian.com/media/2018/feb/25/bbcs-steph-mcgovern-says-she-would-earn-more-if-she-was-posher.

2. The word 'spoken' is important here. Language is a lot more than speech, and it would be possible to look at the different varieties, dialects, and even accents that exist in signed languages. But that is a subject for another book. In the meantime, I refer you to Adam Schembri, and Ceil Lucas (eds.), *Sociolinguistics and Deaf Communities* (Cambridge University Press, 2015), doi:10.1017/CBO9781107280298.

3. There is no hiding the fact that, from a global perspective, this book mainly focuses on a narrow segment of language: English. Even more than this, it mainly deals with varieties of English found in the UK, the USA, and Australia. The reason for this is simply that these are the varieties I know best, and the book needs to be a certain length. If I had the knowledge, the time, and the pages, I would do more. But for now, these are my limitations.

4. Having said that, while 'know' is a bit of a stretch, when I was younger, I did a lot of TV extra work. Over the course of this, I once found myself in the cells underneath Salford magistrates court acting as a prison officer for an imprisoned Ray Winstone. The crew had to be out of the location by 5.00 pm and there was one scene left to squeeze in, which involved me escorting Ray to his cell and then actually saying a line. In order to be out of the location in time, it was essential this happened in one take. We did the scene, I said my line, and all was good. At which point Ray turned to me and in full Winstonese said, 'Well done Rob, proper geezer!' Good times.

5. R. B. Le Page and Andrée Tabouret-Keller, *Acts of Identity: Creole-based approaches to language and ethnicity* (Cambridge University Press, 1985).

6. There's a nice online BBC article that discusses popular theories as to the origins of uptalk here: '10 theories on how uptalk originated', BBC News (2014), https://www.bbc.co.uk/news/magazine-28785865.

7. There has been research into this. For example, linguist Jane Stuart-Smith and her team looked at the effects of the British TV soap *EastEnders* on the accent of young people in Glasgow, and did find evidence that might suggest a slight change of some features towards London rather than Glasgow pronunciations. There is a summary,

with a link to the full study here: 'EastEnders Effect: watching TV can change your accent', *Sci News* (2013), http://www.sci-news.com/othersciences/linguistics/science-eastenders-watching-tv-accent-01375.html.

8   Naomi Wolf, 'Young women, give up the vocal fry and reclaim your strong female voice', *The Guardian* (2015), https://www.theguardian.com/commentisfree/2015/jul/24/vocal-fry-strong-female-voice.

Chapter 1

1   For a much more complete history of English, which looks further than just the standard, I strongly recommend David Crystal, *The Stories of English* (Penguin, 2005).

2   This description comes from a really detailed, accessible, and modern account of the subject: Míša Hejná and George Walkden, *A history of English* (Language Science Press, 2022), p.311.

3   Yes, Scots is a language, although people do debate this. As can be seen in a correction to a recent article in *The Guardian* on Robert Burns: 'This article was amended on 17 January 2022. Scots, in which Burns wrote much of his best-known poetry, is widely regarded as a language, not a "dialect" as a previous version described it.' Caroline Davies, 'Robert Burns letters reveal poet was advised not to write in Scots', *The Guardian* (2022), https://www.theguardian.com/books/2022/jan/17/robert-burns-letters-reveal-poet-was-advised-not-to-write-in-scots-dialect.

4   The phonetician John Wells also notes this hypercorrection (not by my grandfather specifically I presume) in his book, *Accents of English*. John C. Wells, *Accents of English: volume 1* (Cambridge University Press, 1982), p.132.

5   William Caxton, *Eneydos* (1490).

6   I actually got promoted to professor in the course of writing this book. Maybe the promotion panel was impressed by my down-to-earth, rugged, southern, home counties accent.

7   David Crystal has written an interesting article on the myths and realities of Samuel Johnson's dictionary, which can be accessed here: David Crystal, *Johnson's Dictionary: myths and realities* (2018), https://www.bl.uk/restoration-18th-century-literature/articles/johnsons-dictionary-myths-and-realities.

8   Samuel Johnson, *The Plan of a Dictionary of the English Language: addressed to the Right Honourable Philip Dormer, Earl of Chesterfield, one of His Majesty's principal secretaries of state*, (J. and P. Knapton, T. Longman and T. Shewell, C. Hitch, A. Millar, and R. Dodsley, 1747), p.4.

9   British Library, 'Johnson's Dictionary 1755', https://www.bl.uk/learning/timeline/item126707.html.

10 Jonathan Swift, *A proposal for correcting, improving and ascertaining the English tongue* (Benj. Tooke, 1712), p.31.

11 John Walker, *A Critical Pronouncing Dictionary and Expositor of the English Language* (G. G. J. and J. Robinson; and T. Cadell, 1791), p.xx.

12 Ibid, p.xiv.

NOTES

13 Charles Dickens, *The Pickwick Papers* (Huge Print Press, 1905).

14 Charles Dickens, *Hard Times* (Dent, 1854).

15 Daniel Jones, *English Pronouncing Dictionary* (Dent, 1917), p.xv.

16 BBC Archive, 'In 1967 John Reith, the first ever Director General of the BBC, spoke to Malcolm Muggeridge about the "BBC Accent". Reith defended his decision to instruct BBC broadcasters to speak in a rather artificial manner, as opposed to their own local dialects.', Twitter, 2022, https://twitter.com/BBCArchive/status/1585220946566127617?s=20&t=mRpzcqsXYHEWKR0zPrbcyQ.

17 For insights into some of the history around these linguistic varieties, I recommend Mark Sebba, *London Jamaican: language system in interaction* (Routledge, 1993).

18 There has been a lot written about MLE. Linguist and slang expert Tony Thorne's blog, 'Language and Innovation', is a good place to start, with insights from Tony and links to lots of accessible media coverage: https://language-and-innovation.com/?s=mle. For the definitive academic account of MLE, try Jenny Cheshire, Paul Kerswill, Sue Fox, and Eivind Torgersen, 'Contact, the feature pool and the speech community: the emergence of Multicultural London English' in *Journal of Sociolinguistics*, 15(2) (2011), pp.151–196.

19 I describe MBE here, along with some examples: https://www.robdrummond.co.uk/multicultural-british-english/.

20 Farhana Alam wrote her fascinating PhD on the wonderfully named Glasgow-Asian accent: Glaswasian. I met Farhana a few times while she was completing this work, and she was an incredibly knowledgeable and kind academic. Sadly, she was living with serious breast cancer at the time, and died on 24 November 2017, aged 36.

21 For a detailed account of the complexity of the relationship between British and American English, I strongly recommend Lynne Murphy, *The Prodigal Tongue: the love-hate relationship between American and British English* (Oneworld, 2018).

22 If you are interested in finding out more about this diversity, then I strongly recommend seeking out two videos made by dialect coach Erik Singer for *WIRED*, which include insights from linguists and language experts Nicole Holliday, Megan Figueroa, Sunn m'Cheaux, and Kalina Newmark. They take you on a fascinating and detailed linguistic journey across the whole country: 'An Expert Gives a Tour of U.S. Accents — (Part One) | WIRED', YouTube, https://youtu.be/H1KP4ztKK0A.

23 For example, Kate Burridge, 'English in Australia' in *The Routledge Handbook of World Englishes* (Routledge, 2010), p.20.

24 Greg Dickson, 'Explainer: the largest language spoken exclusively in Australia — Kriol', *The Conversation*, (2016), https://theconversation.com/explainer-the-largest-language-spoken-exclusively-in-australia-kriol-56286; Celeste Rodriguez Louro and Glenys Dale Collard, '10 ways Aboriginal Australians made English their own', *The Conversation*, (2020), https://theconversation.com/10-ways-aboriginal-australians-made-english-their-own-128219.

25 For a no-nonsense description of Aboriginal English, I can recommend this piece by Sharon Davis, 'Aboriginal English — what isn't it?', IndigenousX (2022), https://indigenousx.com.au/aboriginal-english-what-isnt-it/.

26   'Ee bah gone? How northern accents could be dead in 45 years', *The Telegraph* (2021), https://www.telegraph.co.uk/news/2021/07/28/ee-bah-gone-northern-accents-could-dead-45-years/.

27   There is a well-known biblical story that links the pronunciation of particular sounds to belonging or not belonging to a particular group. *The Book of Judges* describes a battle between the Ephraimites and the Gileadites in which the Ephraimites are defeated. The triumphant Gileadites then set up a blockade across the River Jordan to prevent any remaining Ephraimites from returning to their land. When someone tries to cross, the guards ask them to say the word *shibboleth* (meaning an ear of grain). Because the Ephraimites had no 'sh' sound in their dialect, they would pronounce the word as 'sibboleth'. This exposed them as the enemy, and they were killed. Any passing Gileadites would use the expected 'sh' sound, and pass on through. This is why we have the word *shibboleth* in English today to mean something that distinguishes between groups.

28   You might have noticed that in the first line of this chapter I refer to 'regional' accents. The simple reason for this is because this term is somewhat problematic, at least in the UK. In accent terms, 'regional' does not tend to mean all regions; it tends to mean 'all regions except the south-east of England'. I come from the south-east of England, and my accent is typical of where I am from, but I would almost never be described as having a 'regional' accent. Now, you might think this is unimportant; you might think that it's fairly standard to think of 'regional' as meaning somewhere away from the area of the capital, so why not describe accents in this way? The problem lies in the fact that by labelling some accents as 'regional', we are creating a sense that they are in some way different from what is normal. We are othering them. We are saying that my accent doesn't need a label; it is unremarkable, normal, and 'standard'. Somebody else's accent does need a label, because it is different, not normal, and non- (or sub-?!) standard. I'm not going to continue writing 'regional' as it might get distracting, but feel free to mentally read it that way.

Chapter 2

1   For non-UK readers, BBC Radio 4 is a spoken-word station whose average listener is aged 56 and middle class, whereas BBC Radio 1 is a music station whose target audience is aged 15–29. For younger readers, a radio is the thing your parents and grandparents sometimes listen to. It's kind of like a podcast and music machine, only you have to listen at certain times.

2   The linguist Ella Jeffries looks at this area. For example, Ella Jeffries, 'Preschool children's categorization of speakers by regional accent' in *Language Variation and Change* 31,(3) (2019), pp.329–352, doi:10.1017/S0954394519000176.

3   Firstly, Labov showed that people tend to use more standard features in their speech depending on the type of spoken task in hand. For example, when a task is more 'formal' and requires more attention such as reading a list of words aloud, a British English speaker might use more 't's and fewer glottal stops in words like *cat* and *matter* (Labov actually focused on the pronunciation in American English of 'r' in words such as *car* and *beer*, but this is a good British equivalent). And when a task

NOTES

is less formal and requires less attention, such as a casual conversation, the speaker might revert to using more glottal stops rather than the carefully pronounced 't's. Labov then demonstrated how these changes were neatly stratified according to social class, with the lower social groups using fewer standard forms overall, the higher social groups using the most, but with each group using relatively more standard forms as the formality of the task increased. However, the most interesting finding is that the second highest social group actually overtook the group above in the two most formal contexts. In our British example, this would mean that the speakers in this group pronounced the 't' in words like *but* and *butter* more often than speakers in the social group that was higher than theirs when it came to tasks that required more focus on what was being said. The reason this is interesting is that it demonstrates how some people will overdo things in their attempt to speak what they consider to be 'properly'. This is a slightly different type of hypercorrection from the example of my grandfather and his pronunciation of 'shuggar', but it is along the same lines. It shows how people have an awareness of how they 'should' be speaking in order to come across as more respectable, intelligent, and accurate, even if the result is overexaggerated.

4   Deborah Cameron, *The Myth of Mars and* Venus (Oxford University Press, 2009), https://global.oup.com/academic/product/the-myth-of-mars-and-venus-9780199214471?cc=gb&lang=en&.

5   Incidentally, if you are interested in linguistic myth-busting, I can also recommend Abby Kaplan, *Women Talk More Than Men ... And Other Myths About Language Explained* (Cambridge University Press, 2014).

6   Another interesting study is a recent one by Kara Becker, Sameer ud Dowla Khan, and Lal Zimman. Using the feature of creaky voice as an example, they show how a binary gender approach to the study of language variation is inadequate. Kara Becker, Sameer ud Dowla Khan, and Lal Zimman, 'Beyond binary gender: creaky voice, gender, and the variationist enterprise' in *Language Variation and Change*, 34(2) (2022), pp.215–238.

7   This is simply because this is where much of the research has been carried out, and we should be very wary of generalising findings to other communities.

8   Deborah Cameron and Don Kulick, *Language and Sexuality* (Cambridge University Press, 2003), p.90.

9   Levon focused on two key features — sssibilant duration and increased pitch range, and presented listeners with two sets of four voices. One set contained the original unmanipulated voice of a gay man who had been judged by another group of people as sounding 'extremely gay', followed by the original voice but with a reduced pitch range, then the original voice but with the sibilant duration reduced, then the original voice with both the pitch range and the sibilant duration reduced. The second set of voices started with an unmanipulated voice of someone who sounded 'straight', and which was then adjusted in a similar way as above but extending the pitch range and the sibilant duration. Levon then had participants listen to various combinations of a selection of the voices, along with a few dummy voices to distract from what was going on, and asked them to rate the voices on various scales, one of which was a simple 'straight–gay' scale. He found that while people did tend to rate the 'gay-derived' voices (the ones based on the voice of the original gay speaker) as more or less gay according to the changes in sibilant duration

and pitch range, especially when they had both been adjusted, it did sometimes depend on the order in which people heard the voices. If they heard a gay voice after a few straight ones, they tended to score it as 'more gay'. This is interesting, as it reminds us of the importance of context. Just as you might see a colour and think of it as slightly more blue than green, when you then see it next to something that is definitely green, it suddenly becomes more blue. The same kind of thing happens with our voices.

10. David Thorpe, *Do I Sound Gay?* (2014).

11. David Thorpe, 'Who Sounds Gay?', *New York Times* (2015), https://www.nytimes.com/2015/06/23/opinion/who-sounds-gay.html.

12. Lucy Jones, 'Lesbian Identity Construction' in *The Oxford Handbook of Language and Sexuality* (2018), doi: 10.1093/oxfordhb/9780190212926.013.28.

13. There is some progress happening. See, for example: B. R. Cornelius, *Talkin' Black and Sounding Gay: An Examination of the Construction of a Multiplex Identity via Intraspeaker Variation* (Doctoral dissertation, 2020). Retrieved from https://scholarcommons.sc.edu/etd/6147.

14. For a clear discussion of this point, read the opening chapter of Carmen Fought, *Language and Ethnicity* (Cambridge University Press, 2006), p.3–18.

15. Jenée Desmond-Harris, '11 ways race isn't real', *Vox* (2014), https://www.vox.com/2014/10/10/6943461/race-social-construct-origins-census.

16. Arwa Mahdawi, 'I'm a bit brown. But in America I'm white. Not for much longer', *The Guardian* (2017), https://www.theguardian.com/commentisfree/2017/mar/21/us-census-whiteness-race-colour-middle-east-north-africa-america.

17. Jonathan Rosa and Nelson Flores, 'Unsettling race and language: toward a raciolinguistic perspective' in *Language in Society*, 46(5) (2017), pp.621–647, doi:10.1017/S0047404517000562. See also H. Samy Alim, John R. Rickford, and Arnetha F. Ball, *Raciolinguistics: how language shapes our ideas about race* (Oxford University Press, 2016).

18. The term intersectionality was coined in the sense in which we now understand it by academic and American civil rights advocate, Kimberlé Crenshaw: 'Demarginalizing the Intersection of Race and Sex: A Black Feminist Critique of Antidiscrimination Doctrine, Feminist Theory and Antiracist Politics' in *University of Chicago Legal Forum* 1989(1), article 8.

Chapter 3

1. Erez Levon, Devyani Sharma, and Christian Ilbury, *Speaking Up* (The Sutton Trust, 2022), https://www.suttontrust.com/our-research/speaking-up-accents-social-mobility/.

2. Shiri Lev-Ari and Boaz Keysar, 'Why don't we believe non-native speakers? The influence of accent on credibility' in *Journal of Experimental Social Psychology*, 46(6) (2010), pp.1093–1096.

3. Jason A. Cantone, Leslie N. Martinez, Cynthia Willis-Esqueda and Taija Miller (2019) 'Sounding guilty: How accent bias affects juror judgments of culpability' in *Journal of Ethnicity in Criminal Justice*, 17:3, 228–253, DOI: 10.1080/15377938.2019.1623963.

NOTES

4 Chelsea Ritschel, 'New Zealand named sexiest accent in the world', *Independent* (2019), https://www.independent.co.uk/life-style/sexiest-accent-attractive-new-zealand-voice-ranking-a8891441.html.

5 James Rodger, 'Birmingham accent ranked LEAST attractive in the UK — and even Wolverhampton is higher', *Birmingham Mail* (2019), https://www.birminghammail.co.uk/black-country/brummie-accent-wolverhampton-most-popular-16261123.

6 Scousers have the 'least intelligent and least trustworthy' accent – while Devonians have the friendliest', *Daily Mail* (2013), https://www.dailymail.co.uk/sciencetech/article-2433201/Scousers-intelligent-trustworthy-accent--Devonians-friendliest.html.

7 Frank O'Laughlin, 'Boston accent ranked "most annoying" in America', 7 News Boston, (2022), https://whdh.com/news/boston-accent-ranked-most-annoying-in-america/.

8 Nikolas Coupland and Hywel Bishop, 'Ideologised values for British accents' in *Journal of Sociolinguistics* 11(1) (2007), pp.74–93, https://onlinelibrary.wiley.com/doi/full/10.1111/j.1467-9841.2007.00311.x.

9 Accent Bias Britain, https://accentbiasbritain.org/.

10 Admittedly, there are issues with this technique, the main one being the fact that unless the speaker is genuinely bi-dialectal (naturally has access to two separate accents or dialects), or is a very good voice actor, one of the guises will always run the risk of sounding fake, put on, or exaggerated. I actually used this technique in part of my PhD research, and employed the services of two drama students to help me out. I simply needed them to read a passage using either a general Mancunian accent, or a general London accent. For each speaker, one of these was their natural accent, and one would be performed. In almost every case, when it came to doing the 'other' accent for the first time, they did it in a bizarrely exaggerated way. For the London speaker, their general Mancunian accent turned into a parody of the Gallagher brothers, and for the Manchester speaker, their general London accent took us on a journey through every cockney stereotype you can imagine. We got there eventually (and the drama students were brilliant), but this says something quite important about how specific features of speech are stereotypically associated with particular accents.

11 Marcus Johns, Erica Roscoe, Dr Arianna Giovannini, Amreen Qureshi, and Rachel Baldini, *State of the North 2021/22: powering northern excellence* (Institute for Public Policy Research, 2022), https://www.ippr.org/publication/state-of-the-north-2021-22-powering-northern-excellence.

12 Lippi-Green calls this the 'communicative burden' — something that is usually shared between speaker and listener to enable effective communication. There is often an expectation on the part of the listener that the speaker should carry a greater share of the communicative burden in order to make themselves understood, especially when the listener has a more 'standard' way of speaking and the speaker has a more 'non-standard' way of speaking. In different situations we can choose to either accept or reject our share of the burden. Rosina Lippi-Green, *English with an accent: language, ideology, and discrimination in the United States* (Routledge, 2012), p.74.

13   Although there are perhaps signs of change here too. The Accent Bias Britain project found that younger people in the legal profession were less inclined than older people to agree to the statement: 'People who work in the legal profession are often expected to adjust their accents to fit a professional norm.' https://accentbiasbritain.org/why-look-at-law/.

14   Hashi Mohamed, *People Like Us: what it takes to make it in modern Britain* (Profile Books, 2020), https://profilebooks.com/work/people-like-us/.

15   I originally made these points in a short article for *Counsel* magazine in Jan 2021: Rob Drummond, 'Accent diversity at the Bar', *Counsel* (2021), https://www.counselmagazine.co.uk/articles/accent-diversity-at-the-bar.

16   Katie Edwards, 'Putting the accent on prejudice', Medium (2021), https://katiebedwards.medium.com/putting-the-accent-on-prejudice-a2894d5d0670.

17   Debuk, 'The taming of the shrill', *Language: a feminist guide* (2016), https://debuk.wordpress.com/2016/03/12/the-taming-of-the-shrill/.

18   Casey A. Klofstad, Rindy C. Anderson, and Susan Peters, 'Sounds like a winner: voice pitch influences perception of leadership capacity in both men and women' in *Proceedings of the Royal Society B: Biological Sciences* (2012).

19   Paul Hill, 'Busting the Margaret Thatcher Voice Change Coaching Myth', *Working Voices* (2013), https://www.workingvoices.com/insights/busting-the-margaret-thatcher-voice-coaching-myth.

20   For example: Judith Humphrey, '5 ways women can be heard more at work', *Fast Company* (2018), https://www.fastcompany.com/90256171/5-ways-for-women-can-be-heard-more-at-work. But there are lots and lots of these. Linguist Deborah Cameron wrote a humorous and enlightening blog post on 'How to write a bullshit article about women's language', Language: a feminist guide (2015), https://debuk.wordpress.com/2015/08/03/how-to-write-a-bullshit-article-about-womens-language.

21   Nic Subtirelu, 'Bashing Hillary Clinton's voice: "screeching", "shrieking", and "shrill"', Linguistic Pulse (2016), https://linguisticpulse.com/2016/02/08/bashing-hillary-clintons-voice-screeching-shrieking-and-shrill/.

22   To get an idea of just how common a feature of spoken language creaky voice is, and not just in English, I point you towards Lisa Davidson, 'The versatility of creaky phonation: segmental, prosodic, and sociolinguistic uses in the world's languages' in *Wiley Interdisciplinary Reviews: cognitive science*, *12*(3) (2021).

23   Gretchen McCulloch provides an accessible discussion of this point, with links to existing research: Gretchen McCulloch, 'Move over Shakespeare, teen girls are the real language disruptors', *Quartz* (2015), https://qz.com/474671/move-over-shakespeare-teen-girls-are-the-real-language-disruptors.

24   For example, Monika Cha and Julia Bursten, 'Girl Talk: understanding negative reactions to female vocal fry' in *Hypatia, 36*(1), pp.42–59; Norman Mendoza-Denton, 'The semiotic hitchhiker's guide to creaky voice: circulation and gendered hardcore in a Chicana/o gang persona' in *Journal of Linguistic Anthropology*, 21(2), pp.261–280; and Katherine Dallaston and Gerard Docherty, 'The quantitative prevalence of creaky voice (vocal fry) in varieties of English: a systematic review of the literature' in *PloS one*, 15(3).

NOTES

25 Rindy C. Anderson, Casey A. Klofstad, William J. Mayew, and Mohan Venkatachalam, 'Vocal fry may undermine the success of young women in the labor market' in *PloS one*, 9(5).

26 Linguist Christian DiCanio offers a detailed description of the issues in a blog post on the Language Log website, Christian DiCanio, 'Vocal fry probably doesn't harm your career prospects', *Language Log* (2014), https://languagelog.ldc.upenn.edu/nll/?p=12774.

27 See for example this clip from *Family Guy*: 'Upward Inflection| *Family Guy* [HD]', YouTube, https://www.youtube.com/watch?v=tqNhEzrWQpY. Also, this comedy routine by Will Noonan that combines criticism of the use of uptalk and vocal fry by young women: 'Best Vocal Fry Comedy Routine — Club Comix', YouTube, https://www.youtube.com/watch?v=To0otqt0cQc.

28 A recent example of a young woman being criticised for her speech is the TikTok content creator @kateo4, as described in this article: Victoria Vouloumanos, 'This Woman Went Viral After Responding To A Man Who Called Out Her "Valley Girl Accent," And I've Never Even Thought About Why Women Use Uptalk', *Buzzfeed* (2022), https://www.buzzfeed.com/victoriavouloumanos/tiktok-valley-girl-voice.

29 F. Fasoli, P. Hegarty, and D. M. Frost, 'Stigmatization of "gay-sounding" voices: the role of heterosexual, lesbian, and gay individuals' essentialist beliefs' in *British Journal of Social Psychology*, 60(3) (2021), pp.826–850.

30 András Tilcsik, 'Pride and prejudice: employment discrimination against openly gay men in the United States' in *American Journal of Sociology*, 117(2) (2011), pp.586–626.

31 Issie Lapowsky, 'Paul Graham on Building Companies for Fast Growth', *Inc.*, https://www.inc.com/magazine/201309/issie-lapowsky/how-paul-graham-became-successful.html.

32 Issie Lapowsky, 'Paul Graham Responds to Founder Accents Backlash', *Inc.*, https://www.inc.com/issie-lapowsky/paul-graham-responds-founder-accents-controversy.html.

33 For his written work, see John Baugh, 'Linguistic profiling' in *Black linguistics* (2005), pp.167–180. Routledge. For his spoken work, see John Baugh, 'The Significance of Linguistic Profiling', TEDxEmory (2019), https://www.ted.com/talks/john_baugh_the_significance_of_linguistic_profiling.

34 Thomas Purnell, William Idsardi, and John Baugh, 'Perceptual and Phonetic Experiments on American English Dialect Identification' in *Journal of Language and Social Psychology*, 18(1) (1999), pp.10–30.

35 Kelly E. Wright, 'Housing Policy and Linguistic Profiling: an audit study of three American dialects' in *Language* (2023).

36 Donald L. Rubin, 'Nonlanguage factors affecting undergraduates' judgments of nonnative English-speaking teaching assistants' in *Research in Higher Education*, 33(4) (1992), pp.511–531.

37 Okim Kang, and Donald L. Rubin, 'Reverse linguistic stereotyping: measuring the effect of listener expectations on speech evaluation' in *Journal of Language and Social Psychology*, 28(4), pp.441–456.

38 In the UK, there is currently a campaign to broaden the scope of the 2010 Equality Act to include accent as a protected characteristic, among some others (Equality Act Review: https://www.equalityactreview.co.uk/). In the US, while there is no specific reference to accent discrimination in law, a ban on discrimination based on national origin has been used to successfully challenge foreign accent discrimination in some cases. In Australia, discrimination based on accent can be unlawful, but only when clearly linked to a person's race or ethnicity.

39 Laura L. Paterson, 'Interview with Erin Carrie and Rob Drummond of The Accentism Project' in *Journal of Language and Discrimination*, 3(1) (2019), pp.76–84.

40 'Stop the Bias Report', Tribepad (2021), https://tribepad.com/app/uploads/2022/03/Tribepad-Bias-Report-DIGITAL-2.pdf.

41 In the Manchester Voices project, there is an example of a solicitor from Bolton who talks of her decision some years ago not to pursue a career as a barrister because she didn't feel she would fit in with her working-class background and northern accent. Available here: Manchester Voices, (2021), https://explore.manchestervoices.org/accent-van.

42 This is a good overview of some of the concerns around unconscious bias training: Christine Ro, 'The complicated battle over unconscious-bias training', BBC (2021), https://www.bbc.com/worklife/article/20210326-the-complicated-battle-over-unconscious-bias-training.

43 The Accent Bias Britain project offers information and training along these lines: 'Reducing bias through training', Accent Bias Britain, https://accentbiasbritain.org/training-intervention/; and The Accentism Project has recently started providing its own training to organisations.

44 Rosina Lippi-Green, *English with an accent: Language, ideology, and discrimination in the United States* (Routledge, 2012), p.104.

45 See for example the ongoing work being carried out as part of the Children's Television Project at Tufts University: https://sites.tufts.edu/ctvresearch/. As part of this research, they look at the use of accents in animated TV programmes.

46 Gregory Wakeman, 'Why are there no Russian accents in 'The Death of Stalin'? Armand [sic] Iannucci explains', *Metro* (2018), https://www.metro.us/why-are-there-no-russian-accents-in-the-death-of-stalin-armand-iannucci-explains/.

47 Hello!

48 Ellen E. Jones, 'Jason Isaacs on The Death of Stalin: "Cameron told me it was exactly like what was going on in Downing Street', *The Guardian* (2017), https://www.theguardian.com/film/2017/oct/20/jason-isaacs-on-the-death-of-stalin-cameron-told-me-it-was-exactly-like-what-was-going-on-in-downing-street.

49 I'm acutely embarrassed about this point. Being an academic linguist, I know quite a bit *about* various other languages, but I remain awkwardly monolingual.

50 Haley Richardson, '"This bloke is destroying British humour": GMB viewers mock linguist who claims mimicking a foreign accent is as offensive as using blackface', *Daily Mail* (2021), https://www.dailymail.co.uk/femail/article-9809523/GMB-viewers-mock-linguist-likens-mimicking-foreign-accent-using-blackface.html.

51 In fact, the whole stereotypical character of Apu is problematic: Michael Melamedoff, *The Problem with Apu* (2017) and Jake Nevins, '"Apu was

a tool for kids to go after you": why *The Simpsons* remains problematic', *The Guardian*, https://www.theguardian.com/tv-and-radio/2017/nov/15/problem-with-apu-simpsons-hari-konabolu-documentary.

Chapter 4

1. Stevie Gallacher, '"People seem more ready to push back": Darren McGarvey on politics, class, good coffee and radical change', *The Sunday Post* (2022), https://www.sundaypost.com/fp/darren-mcgarvey-on-politics-class-and-radical-change/?utm_source=twitter.

2. This Wikipedia entry discusses the disputed origins of the observation https://en.wikipedia.org/wiki/A_language_is_a_dialect_with_an_army_and_navy.

3. William Labov, *The Social Stratification of English in New York City*,(Cambridge University Press, 1966).

4. Allan Bell, 'Language Style as Audience Design' in *Language in Society* 13(2) (1984), pp.145–204.

5. The Accent Van was the brainchild of me and my colleague Erin Carrie, as part of a big research project called Manchester Voices. The Accent Van was to all intents and purposes a mobile recording studio which we drove around our local area, inviting people to climb aboard and talk about the way they speak. Andy Burnham saw The Accent Van mark one in 2016; but in 2021 we launched The Accent Van mark two — a sleek black luxury vehicle with tinted windows, comfortable seats, and an endless supply of sweets for our participants. If you think there's anything odd about that set-up, that's on you.

6. Danny Dyer is a professional cockney.

7. Lucrece Grehoua, *Code-Switching* (2020), https://www.bbc.co.uk/programmes/m000ls8x.

8. April Baker-Bell, *Linguistic Justice: Black language, literacy, identity, and pedagogy* (Routledge, 2020).

9. Rosina Lippi-Green, *English with an accent: language, ideology, and discrimination in the United States* (Routledge, 2012), p.66.

10. April Baker-Bell, *Linguistic justice: Black language, literacy, identity, and pedagogy* (Routledge, 2020), p.31.

11. Devyani Sharma, 'Style repertoire and social change in British Asian English' in *Journal of Sociolinguistics*, 15(4) (2011), pp.464–492.

12. Devyani Sharma, and Ben Rampton, 'Lectal focusing in interaction: a new methodology for the study of style variation' in *Journal of English Linguistics*, 43(1) (2014), pp.3–35.

13. Ibid., p.20.

14. Olga Smith and Linda James, *Get Rid of your Accent Part One: the English speech training manual* (Olga Smith BATCS GLOBAL, 2019).

15. Diletta, 'How to get rid of a foreign accent in English: 5 easy steps', *EF* (2021), https://www.ef.com/wwen/blog/language/how-to-get-rid-of-a-foreign-accent-in-english/.

16 Accent Reduction Program, https://accentreductionprograms.com/.

17 Accents Off, https://accentsoff.com/.

18 Accurate English, https://www.accurateenglish.com/.

19 Elizabeth Gatbonton, Pavel Trofimovich, and Michael Magid, 'Learners' ethnic group affiliation and L2 pronunciation accuracy: a sociolinguistic investigation' in *TESOL Quarterly*, 39(3) (2012), pp.421–446.

20 Ingrid Piller, 'Language Ideologies' in *The International Encyclopedia of Language and Social Interaction* (2015).

21 Thomas G. Dyer, *Theodore Roosevelt and the Idea of Race* (LSU Press, 1992), p.134.

22 Josh Halliday and Libby Brooks, 'Johnson pledges to make all immigrants learn English', *The Guardian* (2019), https://www.theguardian.com/politics/2019/jul/05/johnson-pledges-to-make-all-immigrants-learn-english.

23 'English — our national language', Australian Government Department of Home Affairs (2022), https://www.homeaffairs.gov.au/about-us/our-portfolios/social-cohesion/english-our-national-language.

24 There is an interesting debate between two *Times* columnists, Clare Foges and Oliver Kamm, that touches on this point, along with the extent to which we should offer translation services for people who don't speak English. Clare Godes and Oliver Kamm, 'Duel: should all immigrants learn English?', *Prospect* (2016), https://www.prospectmagazine.co.uk/magazine/duel-should-all-immigrants-learn-english.

25 Leighton Andrews, Written Statement — Welsh Government's Welsh Language Annual Report for 2010/11, https://gov.wales/written-statement-welsh-governments-welsh-language-annual-report-2010-11.

26 Jeremy Bowen, 'Being Welsh' in *This Union* (2022), https://www.bbc.co.uk/programmes/m0013r1v.

27 Bethan Harries, Bridget Byrne, and Kitty Lymperopoulou, 'Who identifies as Welsh: national identities and ethnicity in Wales' in *Dynamics of Diversity: evidence from the 2011 census* (2014), http://hummedia.manchester.ac.uk/institutes/code/briefings/dynamicsofdiversity/code-census-briefing-national-identity-wales.pdf.

28 'Inquiry into language learning in Indigenous communities', House of Representatives Standing Committee on Aboriginal and Torres Strait Islander Affairs (2012), https://www.aph.gov.au/Parliamentary_Business/Committees/House_of_Representatives_Committees?url=atsia/languages/report/index.htm.

29 Nic Savage, '"Beautiful": Wallabies sing national anthem in Yugambeh language ahead of England Test', news.com.au (2022), https://www.news.com.au/sport/rugby/beautiful-wallabies-sing-national-anthem-in-yugambeh-language-ahead-of-england-test/news-story/34a9f4a353552fa445b1a8110d73a1d6.

30 Dr Gerald Roche, 'Another example of backlash against Indigenous language revitalization in Australia: News.com.au reporting on the Wallabies singing the national anthem in Yugambeh. 968 comments on Facebook. Let's take a look', Twitter (2022), https://twitter.com/GJosephRoche/status/1546436395886977024?s=20&t=JP_wkXUE9KSvl_jre9WaqA.

31 Dr Cen Williams provides a description of precisely how the term came about in the foreword to E. M. Thomas, et al., *Translanguaging*

in the classroom: a quick reference guide for educators (National Collaborative Resources: Aberystwyth University and Bangor University, 2022), p.6, https://hwb.gov.wales/api/storage/c0e59e12-c1b7-48d4-b6f1-7354f6170ab5/translanguaging-in-the-classroom.pdf. It turns out that the 1980s is as far away to current teenagers as the 1940s was to those of us who spent that decade listening to Adam and the Ants and plating on ZX Spectrums. Time is weird. Bear that in mind if you are one of those people in their 40s or 50s who thinks, 'Yeah kids, I remember what it was like being a teenager – not that much has changed.'

32 An interesting conversation on translanguaging between two key figures in bilingual research: Francois Grosjean and Ofelia Garcia, 'What is Translanguaging?' in *Psychology Today* (2016), https://www.psychologytoday.com/us/blog/life-bilingual/201603/what-is-translanguaging.

33 L Wéi, 'Translanguaging and Code-Switching: what's the difference?', *Oxford University Press Blog* (2018), https://blog.oup.com/2018/05/translanguaging-code-switching-difference/.

34 Khawla Badwan, *Language in a Globalised World* (Springer International Publishing, 2021), p. xiv.

35 Hanan Ben Nafa, 'Code-switching as an evaluative strategy: identity construction among Arabic-English bilinguals in Manchester' (Manchester Metropolitan University, 2018).

36 I should have thought more of it, if only by virtue of what happened to me while training to be a TESOL (Teaching English to Speakers of Other Languages) teacher. As part of the training we had to meet up with a potential student one-to-one, assess their needs, create a lesson based on those needs, and teach them. I paired up with a Danish student who was working in the UK as an au pair. In the course of talking to her, it became clear that not only was her English already very good, she actually knew far more about the language itself (grammar, sentence structure) than I did. I have absolutely no doubt that at that point she would have made a far more competent English language teacher than me, and yet she would not be eligible to apply for the jobs I could apply for on the basis of her not being a native speaker. I'm not at all proud of the fact that I only properly recognised the injustice and inequality around so many areas of language years later. Actually, I am still very much learning.

37 Vijay A. Ramjattan, 'The white native speaker and inequality regimes in the private English language school' in *Intercultural Education* 30(2) (2019), pp.1–15, 10.1080/14675986.2018.1538043.

38 Vijay A. Ramjattan, 'Lacking the Right Aesthetic: everyday employment discrimination in Toronto private language schools' in *Equality, Diversity and Inclusion: an International Journal* 34(8) (2015), pp.692–704, doi:10.1108/EDI-03-2015-0018.

39 Clare Butler, 'Identity and Stammering: negotiating hesitation, side-stepping repetition, and sometimes avoiding deviation' in *Sociology of Health & Illness* 35(7) (2013), pp.1113–1127, doi:10.1111/1467-9566.12025.

40 Zoe McDonald, 'How singing reverses neurological problems with speech', Queensland Brain Institute (2018), https://qbi.uq.edu.au/blog/2018/04/how-singing-reverses-neurological-problems-speech.

41 'Why don't I stutter when I speak with an accent?', Stuttering Treatment and Research Trust, https://www.stuttering.co.nz/news/why-dont-i-stutter-when-i-speak-with-an-accent/.

42 'Disability Etiquette: how to respect people with disabilities', Vantage Mobilities (2016), https://www.vantagemobility.com/blog/disability-etiquette-dos-and-donts.

43 James Brennan, 'Today marks World Stammering Awareness day — One young Irishwoman tells of her challenges with a stammer', *The Liberal* (2021), https://theliberal.ie/today-marks-world-stammering-awareness-day-one-young-irishwoman-tells-of-her-challenges-with-a-stammer/.

44 *Stammer Stories* https://linktr.ee/stammerstories.

45 Barbara Shadden, 'Aphasia as identity theft: theory and practice' in *Aphasiology* 19(3–5), pp.211–223, doi:10.1080/02687930044000697.

46 Grace Hammond, 'Proud Yorkshireman with cerebral palsy has got his accent back thanks to new speech aid voice', *Yorkshire Post* (2021), https://www.yorkshirepost.co.uk/news/people/proud-yorkshireman-with-cerebral-palsy-has-got-his-accent-back-3301978.

47 David Robson, 'The mind-bending effects of foreign accent syndrome', BBC (2015), https://www.bbc.com/future/article/20150513-the-weird-effects-of-foreign-accent-syndrome.

48 Nick Miller, 'Foreign accent syndrome: between two worlds at home in neither' in C. Llamas and D. Watt, (eds.), *Language and Identities* (Edinburgh University Press, 2010), pp.67–75.

Chapter 5

1 Jonathan Harrington, Sallyanne Palethorpe, and Catherine I. Watson, 'Does the Queen speak the Queen's English?' in *Nature* 408 (2000), pp.927–928, p.927.

2 Ibid.

3 There's a joke in there somewhere about first person pronouns and posh people.

4 Gretchen McCulloch, *Because Internet: understanding the new rules of language* (Riverhead Books, 2020), p.44.

5 In her study on 'Jocks' and 'Burnouts' (two polarised social categories in US high schools), Penny Eckert uses the observed width of jean leg as one of the measures of style at her disposal. She shows how this combines with behaviour, makeup, and, crucially, pronunciation of particular language features to create particular identities. Penelope Eckert, *Linguistic Variation as Social Practice*, (Blackwell, 2000), p.65.

6 Norma Mendoza-Denton, *Homegirls: language and cultural practice among Latina youth gangs* (Wiley-Blackwell, 2007).

7 Mark Lungariello, '"Peppa Pig" effect has kids speaking in British accents during pandemic', *New York Post* (2021), https://nypost.com/2021/07/18/peppa-pig-effect-has-kids-speaking-in-british-accents-during-pandemic/.

NOTES

8 Not the technical term, and probably not the term grime artists would use themselves.

9 Hazey's music is actually more drill than grime, but the distinction isn't always clear. And as this is a book about language rather than music, I hope you'll forgive any generalisation.

10 JDZmedia, 'Bugzy Malone [SPITFIRE] | JDZmedia', YouTube, https://www.youtube.com/watch?v=GsGKkfElA8k.

11 Lady Leshurr, 'Lady Leshurr – *Queen's Speech Ep.4*', YouTube, https://www.youtube.com/watch?v=FyodeHtVvkA.

12 You can watch this interview from American radio here: 'Santan Dace Fires Back at Sam L. Jackson Over Racism Comments + Not Knowing He Was on Drake's Album', YouTube, https://youtu.be/yEH6IU7pDOg.

13 Nick Harding, 'Why are so many middle-class children speaking in Jamaican patois? A father of an 11-year-old girl laments a baffling trend', *Daily Mail* (2013), https://www.dailymail.co.uk/femail/article-2453613/Why-middle-class-children-speaking-Jamaican-patois-A-father-11-year-old-girl-laments-baffling-trend.html.

14 Peter Sokolowski, 'Most English speakers accept the fact that the language changes over time, but don't accept the changes made in their own time.', Twitter, https://twitter.com/PeterSokolowski/status/321693225377230849?s=20&t=vo5AFjmAiUYb32mkSgM_TA.

15 John McWhorter, 'Txtng is killing language. JK!!!', TEDx (2013), https://www.ted.com/talks/john_mcwhorter_txtng_is_killing_language_jk.

16 This is a funny situation to be in as a sociolinguistically minded parent, and I've experienced it myself. I spend a lot of my time talking, writing, and teaching about the fact that language variation is completely normal, that all ways of speaking are valid, and that there are often equally sophisticated rules governing their use. And then one of my teenage children says something in a way that I just know will result in them being judged negatively be others. What do I do? I can't 'correct' them, as that would mean adopting the same behaviour that I so readily criticise in others. It's the paradox of the sociolinguist parent! All you can do is take the approach I recommend for teachers dealing with this in their classrooms — make the person aware that in some situations they might be judged for speaking in this way, explain why, and then spend the rest of your time challenging the ideologies that allow that judgement to happen. Basically, give the individual the awareness and understanding to then enable them to behave as they see fit. They can choose to challenge or adapt, but at least they know some of the background as to why they are in that situation.

17 The avocado on toast story originated from an interview with Australian real estate mogul Tim Gurner in 2017: Sam Levin, 'Millionaire tells millennials: if you want a house, stop buying avocado toast', *The Guardian* (2017), https://www.theguardian.com/lifeandstyle/2017/may/15/australian-millionaire-millennials-avocado-toast-house. The Netflix subscription perspective came from TV presenter Kirsty Allsopp in 2022: Alice Dear, 'Kirstie Allsopp says youngsters can afford a house if they give up Netflix, coffee and the gym', *Heart* (2022), https://www.heart.co.uk/showbiz/celebrities/kirstie-allsopp-young-people-afford-buy-house-gym-netflix-coffee/.

18 I'm not going to link to specific examples of this kind of approach as I don't particularly want to name and shame anyone. But you will just have to trust me that such policies exist in some classrooms and schools.

19 This isn't to suggest that it's only English teachers who can have this knowledge and awareness, simply that they are perhaps more likely to have come across it as part of their education. As I've said elsewhere, I think some kind of sociolinguistics education should be mandatory for anyone who has to deal with any people in any form (so basically, all of us). And this isn't simply to keep me and my friends in work, rather I genuinely think the world would be a better place if people knew just a bit more about how we communicate.

20 Paul Baker, 'A brief history of Polari: the curious after-life of the dead language for gay men', *The Conversation* (2017), https://theconversation.com/a-brief-history-of-polari-the-curious-after-life-of-the-dead-language-for-gay-men-72599. To celebrate 50 years of Pride in 2022, Transport for London put up posters around its transport network using Polari. You can see some of them here: Alex Sims, 'TfL is putting up some very special LGBTQ+ posters to celebrate 50 years of Pride', *TimeOut* (2022), https://www.timeout.com/london/news/tfl-is-putting-up-some-very-special-lgbtq-posters-to-celebrate-50-years-of-pride-063022.

21 Devan McGuinness, 'A parent's guide to teen slang', *The Week* (2019), https://theweek.com/articles/880094/parents-guide-teen-slang.

22 I will do this only briefly here, as this is a book primarily about spoken language; however, for a thorough and brilliantly entertaining description of this area, I strongly recommend the book by Gretchen McCulloch, *Because Internet: understanding the new rules of language* (Riverhead Books, 2020).

23 Ibid., p.73.

24 Roger Hewitt, *White Talk, Black Talk: inter-racial friendship and communication amongst adolescents* (Cambridge University Press, 1986), p.102.

25 Shades of Noir, https://shadesofnoir.org.uk/the-black-cent/.

26 Sydnee Thompson, 'So Much Modern Slang Is AAVE. Here's How Language Appropriation Erases The Influence Of Black Culture', *BuzzFeed News* (2021), https://www.buzzfeednews.com/article/sydneethompson/aave-language-appropriation; Adia Ayanna, 'TikTok Language: what's up with the Misuse of AAVE?', Medium (2021), https://medium.com/the-comeback-of-culture/tiktok-language-whats-up-with-the-misuse-of-aave-e1f19c6c75b3.

27 Imani Benberry, 'Dear Non-Black People, AAVE Is Not "Stan" or "Internet Culture"', *Study Breaks* (2020), https://studybreaks.com/thoughts/aave-not-stan-culture/.

28 Some of the features they looked at were associated very specifically with a particular area — for example, the final vowel in words such as *happy* can be pronounced a bit like 'happi' in some areas, and even like 'happeh' in others — while some were more widespread and simply happen to be used in northern England along with other areas — for example pronouncing 'th' as 'f' in words such as *three* or *both*. In order to make the link between the spellings that were used and the geographic locations in question, the researchers only looked at tweets which had been geo-tagged, meaning that the user had allowed Twitter to record where they were when the tweet was sent. They then looked

at which respellings were used in which areas and found some consistent patterns. For example, tweets with respellings of words such as *city*: 'citeh', and *funny*: 'funneh' were more frequent in the north-west of England, where that accent feature can most commonly be found. A. Nini, G. Bailey, D. Guo, and J. Grieve, 'The graphical representation of phonological dialect features of the North of England on social media' in P. Honeybone and W. Maguire (eds.), *Dialect Writing and the North of England* (2020), pp.266–296.

29 E. Jamieson and Sadie Ryan, 'How Twitter is helping the Scots language thrive in the 21st century', *The Conversation* (2019), https://theconversation.com/how-twitter-is-helping-the-scots-language-thrive-in-the-21st-century-121783.

30 Matthew, 'I deh trust the dentist when they start talking in code about your teeth to their wee pal, you got suhin to say say it to ma face prick', Twitter, https://twitter.com/matthewlenniex/status/809471882835750913?s=20&t=m8z0AxNnkRqcyRlBcEwcpw.

31 'People Are Trying To Tweet With "British" Accents And It's Hilarious', *The Language Nerds*, https://thelanguagenerds.com/2021/people-are-trying-to-tweet-with-british-accents-and-its-hilarious/.

32 V, 'British people be like munday, chewsday, wensday, thuhsday, FROIday, sa-a-day, Sunday', Twitter, https://twitter.com/spacekittens420/status/1245281210722476033?s=20&t=FdoeDNpbL_ZTOdzaLc3nuw.

Acknowledgements

I've loved writing this book. However, it wouldn't have seen the light of day without some excellent people behind the scenes. I'd like to thank my agent, Doug Young, who patiently steered me through the process of developing a conversation in a café in St Albans into a viable book proposal and beyond. I'd like to thank everyone at Scribe, past and present, who has been involved in making the book happen, but particularly Molly Slight, Laura Ali, Adam Howard, Sarah Braybrooke, and Aoife Datta. The book is as good as it is because of your insights. Big thanks to Dan Clayton and Maya Drummond for reading earlier drafts and making valuable suggestions. Thanks also to Vanessa Plaister for some valuable advice around inclusivity. And thanks to the teachers who took the time to talk to me about experiences of accent bias and discrimination. In fact, thanks to all the people who have worked on, taken part in, or engaged with the various research projects that have informed my thinking around spoken language and identity. I'm thinking in particular of Erin Carrie, Holly Dann, Sadie Ryan, Sarah Tasker, Susan Dray, Amanda Cole, Dan Clayton, Ian Cushing, John Bellamy, and Khawla Badwan.

On a more personal note, I had a touch of cancer in the course of writing this book, so immeasurable thanks go to the staff at The Christie and other parts of the NHS for sorting me out so expertly and so kindly. I clearly remember explaining the content of the book in great detail to a wonderful Healthcare Assistant who was thoughtfully trying to distract me from what was going on during a particularly grim procedure. Thank you for sounding interested.

But most of all I would like to thank my family: my wife Lynda, and our three children Maya, Cassia, and Isaac. I'd like to say that I couldn't have written this book without you, but we all know that wouldn't strictly be true; I would probably have done it a lot sooner. However, every other aspect of my life would have been so, so dull. Love you loads, and thanks for being there when I needed you.